PLEIADIAN CODE
I

THE GREAT SOUL RESCUE

EVA MARQUEZ

Disclaimer: This book is not intended as a substitute for the medical advice of physicians. The reader should regularly consult a physician in matters relating to his/her health and particularly with respect to any symptoms that may require diagnosis or medical attention.

DEDICATION

Although we are all different, we share the same goal of serving humanity. Even though we may speak different languages, our hearts speak the same language of unconditional love.

This book is dedicated to everyone who speaks the universal language of unconditional love.

ACKNOWLEDGEMENTS

Blessings come into our lives in many forms and when we least expect them. Accepting the Pleiadians as a part of my family became the biggest blessing I could ask for. It opened the door to infinite possibilities for me and everyone I met on this journey who was brave enough to walk through this door with the Pleiadians into the infinite playground we call life.

Thank you to all my friends and clients. You were my inspiration to write this book. May you be blessed with happiness, good health, abundance, and always surrounded by unconditional love.

I am grateful to all my Pleiadian team editors. Katie Thicke for her first edit and breathing sense into my writing (as you already know, English is my second language, and it could be messy at times), for encouraging me to write when I felt stuck, for her eagerness to listen to the story from different angles, and for asking the Pleiadians many questions.

I am grateful to my family for patiently editing the second and third drafts, living through this story, and the many wonderful conversations that were born from it. I will cherish those moments forever.

I want to express my deepest gratitude to my friend and true teacher, Ann, whom I have known for many lifetimes. She helped me remember the love of God that I was so afraid to embrace. The Pleiadians did not tell me that she is a frequency holder of God's unconditional love and peace; they just skillfully arranged that we would walk the same path for a while so I could let go of my human fears and freely choose to embody the same frequency. The Pleiadian Code I came as a download during one of our visits. She taught me about recognizing and healing life patterns, which I share with you in this book.

I sincerely appreciate David R. Hawkins for writing the book "The Eye of the I, From Which Nothing is Hidden." The Pleiadians guided me to study the Map of Consciousness that David Hawkins shared in his book.

I am thankful to Renata Jokl for her friendship. Her acupuncturist training took us on many meditation journeys that we could talk about for a long time while enjoying the delicious breakfast she always makes for us.

Thank you to all my Charleston soul family. Those who still live here, those who have moved away, and those who have passed on to the other side. You are my soul family. I am grateful for our personal talks, our alien talks, our healing circle, and the potlucks and gatherings we have shared. I love you all unconditionally.

Thank you to Michael Nagula, AMRA Publishing, and their amazing team for all the opportunities they give to writers. The Pleiadians and I are grateful for all you do, not only for us but for everyone.

Table of Contents

FOREWORD

Love is the essence of your being. Love is the miracle cure that will help you heal. Love is a gateway toward your journey to the stars.

The Pleiadian Code I is a tool for sifting through personal and global history to better understand who you truly are. Additionally, it will guide you in turning your inner compass toward your soul-healing journey and assist you in returning to the stars where you came from, to the Universe, when you are ready.

Everything is energy. Everything that has ever existed has an energy imprint. You cannot destroy that energy but move it or transform it. Moreover, all the emerging energy imprints are recorded and can be accessed from the Universal Mind. Anyone seeking spiritual growth can access these recordings to break free from fear patterns. Part of the knowledge from those recordings is shared in this book.

In life, you will encounter different kinds and intensities of fear. This is due to the age-old fact that fear is meant to keep you under control to help you survive. Unconditional love is the only true opposite of fear. The idea of unconditional love is unnatural in the fear mindset. Love must be discovered and set as a new possible mindset program to overcome this fear.

At the moment, the only way to find the state of unconditional love is to release the negative emotions trapped in the lowest part of one's subconscious mind. The negative emotions may be denial, anger, jealousy, guilt, despair, blame, hate, etc. This will open the door to the state of unconditional love. One could say that love is born out of fear if one must surpass the state of fear before surrendering to the mindset of unconditional love.

The Source/Universe/Creator will be called God in this book. The word God has been misused throughout your history, often to keep you in fear. This is so that those falsely claiming to be superior Gods can easily control you. However, the word God holds a high frequency and is full of power. This frequency doubles as the essence of your being.

God, or the frequency that the word contains, exists in everything. It is within darkness just as it is in light. It represents all of us. This energy created the Pleiadians just as it created you. Everything is created equally from what is referred to as God in this book. God has no defined emotion, character, shape, color, or sound. GOD JUST IS! God can be anything you want it to be. We all came from the same God, just as we are on similar journeys back to God.

On your journey back to the Universe, you may even stop on planets such as Pleiades since these planets were once home to you long ago. As all journeys contain the original purpose of gaining new experiences, we are honored to be walking on your journey alongside you.

With Unconditional Love ~ The Pleiadians

CHAPTER 1

TWIN FLAMES

God was peaceful in its realm. God's energy calmly spread above the dramatic clouds of light and dark, and unconditional love was poured into these clouds.

God loves all its creations because they are all created with the same energy, the energy of oneness. We, Pleiadians included, are all children of the same Universe. We only take on personalities and characteristics after we separate from God. God hears all our pleas.

God heard all those benevolent extraterrestrial beings who felt they needed to separate more to be in the light because they believed it was the best. God also heard all those malevolent beings who thought they needed to conquer all because dark is the best. God does not judge, and God does not pick favorites. So, the energy we call God sent out a frequency of unconditional love to heighten both polarities equally with the intention that opposites will attract. This creates the union of twin flames to end separation.

Tia-La and Aro, Akashic Record

This is a story from a long time ago when our galaxy was in a constant state of war because the Alliance of the Dark and the Alliance of the Light lived in separation, with a firm belief that one was better than the other.

Tia-La was a beautiful Sirian princess living in a secluded area of Sirius A with her family and friends. Her heart swelled joyfully as she strolled through the enchanting gardens that embraced her ancestral home. She perfectly embodied the energy of love, peace, and innocence. She was like a pure white rose with droplets of morning dew glistening in the early sun. Her energy reflected in her ever-present visible aura as a shimmering silver glow. Tia-La was full of light. She was kind, loving, patient, gentle and understanding. She spent most of her time teaching children and assisting them to develop their imagination, creativity, telepathy, and inner intuition. She was as graceful as she was wise. Everyone adored her. Her Sirian mission was to be of light, to teach, and to be a Wisdom Keeper like her ancient Sirian ancestors.

On Sirius A, Tia-La grew up living in a Utopia, believing everything was perfect. She was a direct descendant of a very old and influential Sirian family. Thus, she held the ancient bloodline, the original Sirian DNA. Under these circumstances, her family concluded that holding back information about lower vibrations

5

would benefit her as she was considered the future of the Sirian race. Growing up, she had never heard about wars, the Alliance of the Dark, or struggles in the Universe. On occasion, she traveled with her family to Pleiades and Andromeda. Her family always arranged a beautiful and peaceful stay without interfering with the galactic news.

Sirius, Andromeda, and Pleiades are soul planets connected by the power of a trinity. The energy of the trinity acts as a catalyst and is respected across the Universe. For this reason, it is a universal war-free zone. God established this a long time ago, and everyone obeys this.

One of the most honorable Sirian duties is being a scribe in the Akashic Records. Being a scribe is a choice. Tia-La was ambitious and proud to be Sirian. She loved to study history and could not wait until she could apply for a position as a scribe to honorably fulfill her Sirian duties. Naturally, her overprotective family tried to discourage her from accepting this duty because, as a scribe in the Akashic records, she would be exposed to the truth about the Universe and become aware of the severe troubles. Nevertheless, her family could not stop her, so they secretly arranged that she would only be assigned scribe jobs connected to the highest vibrations in history. This worked for a little while.

One day, when everyone was comfortable thinking, she would not be exposed during her scribing assignments, she opened the forbidden records regarding the wars. The shock of the news left her confused. How could she not have known? How come no one told her? Tia-La experienced anger and turmoil for the first time, leading to original discontent in her soul. She kept her discovery a secret so that she could have time to process it in her mind.

The Akashic Records contain a substantial amount of recorded history. Some records also encode the forms of living art energy. For example, it's like adding a video clip to a news article. Living art energy means that the energy of the moment of its capture is always present. When you look at a photograph encoded with living art energy, it would appear as a few seconds of video showing the person or scene at the moment that was captured.

One of these pictures grabbed Tia-La's attention. She read in length about a dark Orion warrior named Aro. He was fearless, arrogant, and cold. She imagined him as a hideous man in an old, sickening body. She was disgusted by all the wars he led, the planets he conquered, and the things he did. Despite this, she asked herself why she was intrigued to read more about his quests. Then she came across a living art picture of him. The picture caught her completely off guard. She did not know what to think! She stared into the most intense, beautiful, piercing light blue eyes that were looking straight back at her. They stared deep into her soul, making her feel like he could read her thoughts. It felt like she knew those eyes! Perplexed, she stared at the handsome warrior with a light tone, perfect skin, and prominent cheekbones. He had dark, wavy, slicked-back hair, dramatic eyebrows arching over sharp, piercing eyes, and full lips that could talk anyone into anything. Quickly, she stopped herself and tore her eyes from the picture. Her heart was beating so fast; she was confused by those eyes. They were not as evil as she imagined him to be. There was something different about him. Then there was the way the news had described him. But there was something in those eyes, something that spoke to her.

This story happened when Orion was under the guidance of the Dark Alliance. The Orion warrior Aro incarnated into a family of dark. He never questioned it. He could not remember his parents, only his strict military training. You had to be tough to survive, and he was the toughest. Aro did not care to learn about God or that we all came from the same place and chose our path as a learning experience. He did not know he was trapped in one part of duality and genuinely believed his mission was to destroy and conquer. He did not know happiness or love and did not worry about it. Male energy had a need that needed to be fulfilled by taking the right actions. That was his belief. After all, that was how he was raised. Genuinely ignorant, Aro lived on the edge and was emotionally dormant. According to him, all was good.

One day, everything changed. He had a dream. In the dream, he walked into a garden full of beautiful flowers, and for once in his lifetime, he felt relaxed and safe. He did not know what beauty was, but these flowers and their magical scent did something to his senses that he could not understand. Then he saw her walking down the path. Her tall, slender figure moved with such elegance, enveloped in a silver shimmering glow, her rich brown hair falling over her shoulders. He felt the urge to touch her to see if she was real. She locked her golden eyes with his and smiled at him. Her eyes were soft and compassionate. He felt this warm feeling spreading over his chest. She looked like a delicate flower. Something inside of him wanted to have this flower for himself.

In his bed, his sleeping body moved restlessly. He murmured her name in his dream, Tia-La, like he knew her forever. At that moment, their souls connected like two magnets of different polarities, like they always belonged together. The light and dark attracted one another, and the twin flame was born.

Time passed quickly after Tia-La learned about Aro. She developed a fascination for the Orion warrior. She followed his many journeys with the records that came in. She saw how menacing he was, but also recognized a hidden kindness within him that she knew no one else noticed. Aro worked hard on covering it up. There were beings whose lives he had spared and places that could have been ruined and damaged forever but were left standing. Tia-La seemed to know he was not all dark. She would gaze into his eyes every day, and her aura filled with the pink energy of love. Her heart fluttered when he looked back at her from the pictures, and she thought it was just her imagination.

Aro's dreams of this beautiful Tia-La intensified and drove him crazy. On top of it all, he started to slowly change. He felt empathy toward places and people whom he had easily harmed in the past. Empathy was not a good thing to thrive on in the Dark Alliance, so he had to hide his occasional act of kindness very well. This irritated him greatly! Why was he changing? What happened to him? Was he sick? Little did he understand he was awaking into the light.

Tia-La, on the other hand, was awakening into the dark. She experienced new feelings, such as being upset, anxious, angry, and wanting the wars to end. She also realized she was in love with Aro but could not help it. She desired to help him. Tia-La knew what love was. She grew up surrounded by love and believed that if she could meet Aro and explain to him that love is the highest energy, all these ridiculous wars would end. He would end them, and she would help him. She made it her mission to find Aro, to teach him about love, and to stop the wars.

Since Tia-La stepped into her dark side, she no longer listened to God, meditated over her decisions, or was driven by needy love and desire. This made her naïve and narrowed her thoughts. Somehow, she did not realize that Aro was not the only warrior causing the wars. Aro was a part of the Dark Alliance and very much under the command of others.

Needy love can blind you, while unconditional love can heal you.

Tia-La told her family about her discovery in the Akashic records. She withheld her secret of being in love with Aro (never before did she have any secrets; that is dark-sided energy). Of course, they tried to discourage her from any actions. She declared that she would apply to the Council of Light for a position to be a peacekeeper among other star nations. She thought she would receive this position because she was a princess. She was wrong. Her application was denied. The Council of Light would not give her the job just because she was a princess.

By this point, Tia-La was tainted with dark energy and desired to change the Universe according to what she thought was right. Aro was tainted with light energy. He wanted changes in his life, and their polarities were calling to each other. So Tia-La took faith into her own hands and secretly left to find this warrior.

She believed that if she could convince him to stop all the wars and declare peace across the Universe, they would both be heroes, fall madly in love, and live happily ever after. It was a perfect plan.

Unfortunately, soon after her secret departure, she was captured by dark forces from Mintaka, and her freedom was gone. The high officials recognized that she was a royal princess from Sirius and held her hostage. At the same time, Aro's dreams of the beautiful princess became more intense. Intuitively, he felt guided to do some business in Mintaka, where Tia-La was being held captive synchronously. He was a high-ranking commander often associated with the high official council.

In his meeting with the Dark Alliance intelligence officials, he was told about the capture of the Sirian princess. His heart skipped a beat, his gut clenched like someone would punch it, but his face remained hard as stone. Who is this princess, he wondered in his mind. Why is his body reacting?

At the first opportunity he had, he went to see this princess. He instantly recognized the woman from his dreams with one look at her face. Could that be? Could she be real? The woman who haunted his dreams was standing before him, looking at him like she knew him as intimately as he knew her. Her eyes searched his face with hope. He dared not show recognition or compassion for her before the guards, so he left. He was furious. Tia-La was confused, and impatience stirred inside her. Their eyes had met for a brief moment. She knew he recognized her, or was she just imagining it? His face showed no emotions; he did not say a word and walked away as fast as he had come in.

Why was this happening to him? Aro shook his head in an attempt to clear it. He used to be content; he did not care about anything. He was doing his job and pretty ignorant of all feelings until she came to him in his dreams. She opened something within him that he never knew existed. He began to care for all those planets he was supposed to conquer. Now, he had compassion toward innocent beings and a need for her. He decided it was all her fault. He hated her at that moment, and he hated himself.

At the meeting, he learned that the Dark Alliance was planning to sell Tia-La to the highest bidder. He knew her future would be as dark as his soul before he started to dream about her. If he bought her, it would be highly suspicious among his kind. He could not just buy her and live happily ever after. He thought that was not his destiny, but his mind worked at the speed of light on a grand plan. The only way to rescue her would be by creating a distraction. And the only way he could leave his current life behind would be to fake his own death.

Aro experienced a great awakening. The shock of needing to save Tia-La opened his eyes and his mind to new realizations. He was sick and tired of wars that never ended, seeing that it was all about conquering or being conquered and knowing that no one intended to end this. The power of love opened his eyes, but Aro did not know it yet. Planning took a few days. He could not visit or let her know she would soon be safe. If he did it, it would raise great suspicion, and this was killing him inside. His mind was clouded with worries, and he could not see her in his dreams. For the first time in his life, guilt gnawed at his insides. He decided to betray his own people to save Tia-La.

Secretly, he told the enemy how they could invade the headquarters in Mintaka. When the invasion started, he cleverly offered to secure the high-profile prisoner. It was granted to him without any suspicion. Shortly after he entered the building where Tia-La was held captive, the building exploded, and all that was left was dust. The master plan included explosions where everyone believed that they all died, unfortunately.

As soon as he entered the building, he killed all the guards and ushered her onboard an unmarked spaceship before the explosion happened. Confusion about the invasion and dust from the blast covered their escape, and they were not detected. Finally, they were together and traveled into the unknown at the speed of light. They had plenty of time to unravel their feelings for each other, fight, and love each other. They were mirrors of one another, showing one another what each was missing in themselves.

Time came and went, and eventually, they were both lost as to what was to come next.

Each of them had to give up their life. Nothing was like they had imagined it would be. Even though the feelings of passionate love were amazing, there were unhealed soul memories that created unwanted sorrow. Tia-La did not stop the wars, and she missed her family. She felt guilty for leaving without saying goodbye. Now, she would never see them again. Aro lost everything he knew and believed in. He betrayed his people and feared that if the Dark Alliance figured out the truth, they would hunt them down until they were found. He knew very well what they would do to Tia-La, and fears of being unable to protect her turned into nightmares. He also started to feel guilty over the actions he had taken in his life before his awakening.

Their twin love was based on their needs for one another, needs for energies (pieces of puzzles) they each lacked. They gave and took, hurt and healed, loved and hated, pleaded and demanded but did not learn to compromise to meet each other on neutral ground, to be equal.

At last, they agreed to secretly contact Tia-La's family in Sirius to let them know she was still alive. Her family rejoiced at this information, but Tia-La and Aro could not visit Sirius since everyone believed she died. If she miraculously re-surfaced, it would bring great danger to everyone. So they lived in hiding, and their fairy tale life was not as bright as they thought it would be.

Tia-la's family turned to God to ask how to help this couple so they, too, could find their everlasting happiness and peace without having to stay hidden. God guided them to join with the Pleiadians in their Earth project. This project aimed to learn about all aspects of duality, the dark, and the light, to find the path to the house of God. The twin flame couple welcomed this opportunity.

You may ask, did they have to come to Earth to learn this and unify their polarities? The answer is simple: no. There are always multiple choices. If they had followed the guidance of God instead of their ego since the first realization of their connection, they would have been guided on how to achieve their union, how to stop wars, and how to live in harmony and peace. Now, on Earth, they received the opportunity to learn the meaning of the old saying, "Let go and let God."

They arrived during the Atlantean time. Earth density heightens the lower vibration emotions such as shame, guilt, fear, anxiety, desire, etc. That was a significant hurdle for both, which they had not expected. Thankfully, they were welcomed into the Pleiadian soul family of light. Pleiadians are soul healers, and they assisted them in understanding what they were feeling. They helped them see the original hurt/pain in their soul. How did it happen, why did it happen, and how could they transform all these low-density emotions into higher-vibration emotions to heal their soul.

All changes take time, and change occurs only once you are ready to see everything as it is—until you realize that you are the creator of your misery and that only you can change it. You are not the victim; you just believe you are because you are disconnected from your higher self and God.

Tia-La and Aro did feel like victims of their own circumstances. Both were stubborn, believing my way was the right way.

His daily emotional suffering drained Aro because he blamed himself for everything. He needed to be in control over their future, which was unclear. He felt angry often. He hated himself and thought, how could anyone love him? He felt done with life. He had reached the end. He believed that no matter what he did, he could not make Tia-La happy.

Tia-La had frustrations of her own. She loved their new life in Atlantis. She met so many soul brothers and sisters that she felt like she was home on Sirius. She was teaching children again and walking in beautiful gardens. She loved Earth, and she also loved Aro, but their love always faced some serious problems. She wondered why love had to be so painful. She remembered love as the most beautiful, profound energy she had ever experienced. Now, her love was laced with fear and control. She felt that no matter what she did, she could not make Aro happy.

One day, while walking in the garden, she bent down to look at her reflection in the stream. Her silver glow was gone. She was sad and tired. She could see her mistakes and knew no one else to blame but herself. Suddenly, she remembered how she used to talk to God when she was little. Without even thinking about it, her whole story was pouring out with her tears falling into the stream.

That morning, Aro woke up with an intuition to finally surrender. For the first time, he acknowledged his inner self and began to meditate, venturing into the depths of darkness within himself. He no longer fought the urge to forget all he had ever done. He accepted it and all its consequences, even though it would mean his death. He walked through his darkness and witnessed every part of his life. He was sorry, and he cried. He acknowledged all his actions and that which he learned from them. Then he saw a sign, "Forgive yourself and give forgiveness to others." Through inconsolable sobs, he forgave himself, and he forgave others. He did not know how long he was there, how long he cried, or how long it took him to forgive himself. Aro surrendered and accepted his dark side within, with the full knowledge of how destructive it could be.

This led him to a new kind of energy. For the first time in his life, he felt the love of God. He felt surrounded by magnificent benevolent beings from all parts of the Universe, both dark and light in nature. They all shined unconditional love at him. He felt the dark and light unified within him for the first time. There was no need or desire. The love he felt was unconditional. The love opened the end of the tunnel, and light poured in. In this light, the most beautiful being walked in, surrounded by her shimmering silver glow, her white gown gently flowing as she moved, her brown hair fell on her back, her golden eyes smiled, and she called his name. Aro stood up and ran toward Tia-La.

Each of them surrendered. They accepted their light, their dark, and their life circumstances. They forgave each other. They were filled with unconditional love. Their soul shined bright rainbow colors so that other twin flames could follow this path, their twin flame rainbow path of soul healing.

The experience made them whole again. He no longer needed her, she no longer needed him, yet they wanted to be with each other. Their unconditional love was pure, strong, and infinite. They could have easily walked their separate paths feeling the same about one another, wishing the best for one another, no matter the circumstances. They decided to stay together since they both felt an unconditional love for one another. They dedicated their lives together to spread information to and about other twin flames. After all, universal love is the highest frequency. They built the Twin Flame Temple in Atlantis, mirroring the one on Sirius B, and dedicated their energy and life to this sacred journey.

THE TWIN FLAME TEACHING

The twin flame energy intensifies attraction and passion. The energy of twin flames creates wants and needs that are often confused for love, whereas in reality, this energy works as a mirror to show you what you are missing. The intensity of twin flame relationships opens the door to finding the missing pieces of oneself and the opportunities for soul healing. The twin flame energy helps us see the opposite sides in ourselves, the dark and the light within us, which we are meant to unify. Thereupon, the needy love of the twin flame could be transcended into unconditional love, oneness, and wholeness. This is only after both polarities accept one another the way they are and surrender to the will of God instead of their own choice.

You cannot change someone to be how you want them to be; you can accept them as they are. Respect their soul choices and love them unconditionally.

Ask yourself, what is it that you are missing? What triggers you? Instead of wanting to change another, change yourself. Work on yourself and identify your weaknesses and your blockages. Heal your soul, find self-unconditional love, and observe how your change impacts the other person.

Go within yourself often, do not be afraid to open the door of dark and light, and accept both sides as equal forces. Naturally, you fear darkness, but darkness is a natural part of you, and accepting it will open the hidden door to the ultimate power you have and are afraid of. Just like God, you can create or destroy with a simple thought. It depends on what you choose. The one who holds the power has integrity and is aligned to the higher self and God. Transcending the duality into oneness and fully embodying the oneness within is the key to the ultimate soul power.

EDUARDO AND NATALIA

In 2018, I worked with my client Eduardo to heal his past relationship. The story you just read was from Eduardo's Akashic Record.

Eduardo (Aro) ended a five-year marriage with his ex-wife, Natalia (Tia-La), on terrible terms. Both were stubborn and angry and blamed one another for the failure. Eduardo awakened into spirituality through tremendous soul suffering and problems in his business. He was willing to address his darkness to heal whatever was between them for the sake of their two young children.

As we worked together, he began to see his somewhat inflated ego. To my surprise, he turned his stubbornness into the most positive willpower you could imagine, which propelled him on his healing journey.

The beginning of his conscious journey was painful and problematic. There were many ups and downs. He started to read spiritual books that interested him, applied the knowledge he learned, and slowly started to change. The most phenomenal part was that his whole family began to heal as he changed. His mother, sister, and people around him began to change and speak the truth. He even began to heal his business and had many new ideas.

Eduardo accepted that his ex-wife and he would walk separate paths. This was life changing. He understood unconditional love and that he could love Natalia unconditionally. He could see her get married to another man. He could support her when needed and have a magnificent, happy life without jealousy, anger, guilt, or blame. He could be an excellent father to his children and have a fantastic business based on integrity, honesty, abundance, success, and mutual benefit for all involved.

And that is the power of a healed twin flame love. It manifests in your life to help you, not to harm you.

You may wonder, if Aro healed his soul in Atlantis, why did this repeat in this lifetime?

After the fall of Atlantis, those who decided to stay on Earth to be in service (like Tia-La and Aro) eventually fell into the trap of reincarnation and suffered spiritual amnesia.

You are living in the momentum of energy that is highly supportive of remembering who you truly are, but you need a reminder. We (Pleiadians) call it a trigger. Triggers offset suffering, intending to awaken ancient memories. To fully comprehend these memories, you are required to heal your soul.

Triggers are negotiated among souls before birth. You know these as soul contracts. Before this lifetime,

Eduardo made a soul contract with Natalia in which they would find each other to recreate all the passion, attraction, and unhappiness created by the needs and wants of the twin flame. They agreed to have two children together because their love for their children will help them make peace with each other, which will also positively contribute to their children's soul contract.

In their soul contract for their current lifetime, they each agreed to embody the energy of wholeness and unconditional love to become frequency holders for others, not as a couple, but as separate whole individuals to demonstrate to others that you do not have to live a life in limited misery. It is expected to fall in love, learn from it, grow from it, and fall out of love. No one is bound to one person forever just because they feel passion, which later turns into jealousy and a need to control one another. They needed to recreate their experience to remember the ancient soul memories that would serve them (and others) in their life mission.

TRUE LOVE

When finding the right person, the passion and attraction one feels is the energy of a missing piece of the puzzle, something one subconsciously thinks one wants or needs.

Next time you feel attracted to someone, just ask yourself what attracts you the most to this person? It could be that he/she is outspoken, and you are shy and secretly wish to be a good speaker. Maybe it is a beautiful body, and you secretly hope that your body was more attractive. Perhaps it is generosity, and you secretly wish you were more generous. It can be anything. Be honest with yourself, and before you fall in love, first give yourself what you are attracted to. For example, if you are shy, then work on your confidence. Once you find your confidence and are still attracted to this person, that could be true love that will last instead of just an attraction to something you subconsciously need or want.

In conclusion, be brave. Refrain from confusing love for something you are missing. If you meet your twin flame, find your missing pieces, change yourself, and see if your relationship develops into true unconditional love. Ask yourself if it is a happily ever after or if this was just another opportunity to find what you wanted or needed for your soul healing. Life is too short to spend it being heartbroken, bitter, angry, or sad.

CHAPTER 2

SOUL, EGO, AND YOU

The soul is part of God, as the ego is part of the human, and you are part of both. Throughout this book, we will use the word ego to define your human energy and the word soul to describe your God's energy. ~ Pleiadians

SOUL

When a baby is conceived, the first organ to develop is the heart. The heart represents the unique and physical you, a wild card with infinite possibilities. The heart is directly interconnected with the soul for each incarnation. You will have a different heart within a different body but the same soul for each incarnation.

Imagine a closet full of outfits (bodies), each designed with a personality that will make you believe you control your destiny. It is important to understand that being in a body can feel limiting, uncomfortable, and challenging.

In three-dimensional reality, you are not supposed to fully awake and become aware of who you are. If you do, you will desire healing. If you heal your soul, you will never want to return to Earth by your own free will, and what you will have is a closet full of unworn outfits.

The soul and ego begin their journey at the moment of conception. The energy for new life already exists behind the scenes. With your first breath, your soul and ego walk hand in hand into your body. Both are present throughout your whole life.

The soul is connected to your higher self. The higher self, which contains memories of your past lives (extraterrestrial included), is connected to God's oneness. The ego is connected to the Earth's energy source, which we call the Surrogate God, which was genetically engineered to reflect God and was eventually misused (you will learn more about this later). Your higher intelligent mind is artificially blocked and replaced by its lower version of the ego. When you figure this out in one lifetime, you will forget it the next time you descend from Heaven to your next incarnation. At the beginning of each incarnation, you are guided to walk across the River of Forgetfulness, which causes your conscious memory to be cloaked. Only a few manage to rush through this river and keep some of their memories intact.

EGO

The ego represents human energy, which is deeply anchored within Earth's energy in the Surrogate God to hold you in the incarnation cycle. The ego is an anchor for your soul, enabling you to thrive in Earth's environment and the physical body. For the time being, it is your helper and your protector.

When the body, soul, and ego meet (notice the trinity of energy), the soul and the ego exchange files containing information about past lives that hold your soul wounds. Imagine two smartphones transferring files by simply taping them together to share the data from one to the other.

The ego perceives soul wounds as possible life threats. The ego's life mission is to protect the soul. In other words, the ego is a life jacket that keeps you alive while the soul is on an adventure. Your higher self is patiently waiting for you to figure out how all this works so that you will stop walking in circles, find healing, become whole, and return home.

The ego is your biggest protector yet your most significant blockage. Its primary job is to help you survive, reproduce, and stay in the incarnation cycle so it can have a meaningful job. It does not care about spirituality, soul growth, or your desire to return home. However, to please you, it will pretend that it cares.

YOU – IN THE BODY

When you consciously awaken and have that big "AHA" moment, you will understand that there is much more out there than your current life. You will suddenly be dealing with two energy forces that will almost constantly compete to be the main navigator of your vessel. You will start to experience huge highs and lows.

Remember that your ego, which strongly identifies with the human you are, has the job description of protecting you at all costs, while your awakened soul has the job description of guiding you on the soul-healing journey as fast as it can. We want you to consciously notice and be aware of these two energy forces. Since Earth is a place of duality, you will always have to identify with two main parties (your human ego and your infinite soul).

THE THREE-WHEELED CAR

Often, we favorably speak of the power of the number three. If you desire to generate transformation, healing, and growth, you must first understand the soul and ego and then add your energy to make three to create the catalyst.
- Your awakened soul is the first.
- The aspect of the ego is the second.

- The physical conscious you make is the third particle.

Combining these three together can generate the transformation you are seeking. We know this is confusing, as we just split one whole being into three parts connected by one heart.

Imagine you are a simple car with three wheels. Each wheel represents one of the above. For most of you, your wheels are going in different directions. You think you are moving, whereas you are just stuck in one place. To reach your destination, you must pay equal attention to each wheel. You just need to learn how to make all three go the same way simultaneously.

The ego and soul take equal turns to be the main driver of your car. This dramatically influences your life, with each turn lasting seven years. What does this mean? When you are in soul years, the soul has more power to control your life journey. It is the most fruitful time to create out of your heart, your soul. You feel creative and more unrestrained. When you are influenced by your ego years, you focus more on your safety and security in your Earth life. You feel more fear. When you become conscious of these patterns, you can easily navigate them and make them work for you positively instead of having these energies sabotaging you.

0 - 7 soul years
7 - 14 ego years

14 - 21 soul years
21 - 28 ego years
28 - 35 soul years
35 - 42 ego years
42 - 49 soul years
49 - 56 ego years
56 - 63 soul years
63 - 70 ego years
70 - 77 soul years
77 - 84 ego years
84 - 91 soul years
91 - 98 ego years
And so on

END OF THE CYCLE

By the end of your physical three-dimensional life, your last heartbeat allows your final breath, allowing the ego and soul to exit the vessel, partially disconnecting from each other. The ego rests in the 3D energy of the Earth, and the soul rests in the 4D Heaven. The symbioses of these two energies could be compared to the twin flame energy of the love/hate, need/want relationship.

If your goal is to end the incarnation cycle, you need to start consciously healing all these parts. You are the third particle and have tremendous power to heal

30

yourself. The physical body is a gift you need to be aware of. It begins with accepting your ego and your soul. Just become best friends with both. Each of them has a story to tell you and could grant you tremendous help.

THE SOUL'S POST-TRAUMATIC STRESS SYNDROME DISORDER

Journeying from one lifetime to another without soul healing poses various problems for the soul and the quality of each life. Being stuck in the incarnation cycle between Earth and what you call Heaven is the biggest one. Throughout your physical life, you often experience various challenges leading to an emotionally broken heart. You may have suffered abuse, poverty, hopelessness, illness, or any misfortune that may torture you, leaving invisible emotional scars on your soul. Only low vibration energies leave marks. If you do not allow yourself to heal these scars in the lifetime they originated in by the end of that life, records of these traumas are sent back with your soul to be written in your Akashic Records. You will carry imprints of them in your next incarnation. When your soul is overloaded by trauma, the soul develops what is called the soul post-traumatic stress disorder (S-PTSD). This results in the soul somehow forgetting that it is part of God. The soul slowly loses its hope and faith. The soul becomes lost, yet it is infinite. This is the current situation of many incarnated souls, depending on how many unhealed lifetimes they have lived since Atlantis. The highest energy to heal the soul is love, which is eternal and infinite.

YOU ARE A SOUL HEALER

Pleiadians are Soul Healers. Pleiadian starseeds are Soul Healers. Earth needs many Soul Healers at this time.

If you feel connected to the Pleiadians or any other star nation, you are one of them. We are your ancestors. You do carry our DNA and have what we like to call special abilities (to make it sound more exciting). That is until you arrive at the realization that there is nothing special about it. It is as normal as someone having blonde or black hair. Our collective mission is to assist Earth and its inhabitants in healing their souls so that they can elevate from the energy of fear into a frequency of unconditional love, ultimately reaching Universal peace. Extraterrestrial or human beings, we are all one. No one is better than the other. Earth is a learning place. You return to this world in different bodies, having different races, colors, or sexual preferences. You may speak different languages and have different spiritual or religious beliefs. You are learning to put your differences aside, preserve this place for others while being one of them, and then return home. One may know more or be more skilled than another; however, anyone can learn if they have the will to do so. Ultimately, WE ARE ALL ONE!

4D IS A TRAP FOR THE SOUL

The fourth-dimension world is a fascinating place but also a trap for the soul. When the soul develops S-PTSD, it ultimately gets stuck in the reincarnation cycle. The rule of Earth is that what happens on Earth has to be healed on Earth. If the trauma has occurred in the physical vessel (body), it has to be healed in/through the physical body. The S-PTSD cannot be healed while the soul is out of the body (after passing away) or rejuvenating in the fourth-dimensional energy (Heaven). Heaven is a beautiful place where you feel like you are on the most fantastic vacation. Your soul experiences ecstatic happiness and peace away from Earth's suffering, where you forget about the original desire to find your way back home to Pleiades or God.

Eventually, the soul will feel pulled by the ego's energy to return to Earth to learn another lesson. Nevertheless, these lessons do not contribute to healing one's conscience, which can complicate things. Often, these lessons can bring about other levels of suffering that create yet another layer of S-PTSD so the soul can happily be trapped in this process of the incarnation cycle forever with a false positive need to keep returning to Earth. It is a "wonderful," never-ending pattern. You are the only one who can break it because you have the power of your physical body and conscious soul! We repeat, "Having a physical body is a gift."

DO NOT PANIC

Stay calm right now. This pattern of reincarnation works fine until you realize that you want to get out of this cycle and are ready to heal your S-PTSD. The Pleiadian Code I opens the vast library within you to discover ancient knowledge of your origin and healing. Knowledge is power, and your power is stored within the soul, guarded by your higher self. Your power will be released to you when your soul is healed. As we mentioned in the previous chapter, power has both polarities, creative and destructive, and you are learning to be master of both of them.

Healing your S-PTSD is a slow journey backward, going from this life to your first one on Earth. We would like to share some healing stories with you so you can find your own. Do not be pushed around by your ego or unhealed soul. Become your own healer instead! Through this book, we will support you with the fifth-dimensional energy of unconditional love. Your assignment is to master self-love, inner strength, and kindness in your third-dimensional body. Remember, S-PTSD has to be healed from and with the energy of the third-dimensional body. Once this is achieved, your soul can quickly move between the third and the fifth-dimensional energy while still in the physical body. This is like your Atlantean ancestors did; they were not bound to the incarnation cycle (being trapped in Heaven) when the soul left its vessel.

There is no shortcut. This journey is like a path on a foggy day. You can only see a few feet ahead of you at a time. You must learn to trust in guidance, feel comfortable in your choices, and trust in the unknown. Trust that the Pleiadians, the Universe, and God have your back. If you ever meet guides that dictate what you should do or flare your ego with some extraordinary past live information, STOP! Or, if they fill you with fear or argue with you, you should think twice about it before starting to work with them.

SIOBHAN, AKASHIC RECORD

Siobhan stood barefoot in the field of wildflowers. She wore a simple peasant top with short sleeves tucked into her ankle-length linen skirt. Seventeen and madly in love, she deeply inhaled the scent of the nearby forest and marveled over the beauty of nature. She felt free, like a bird that could fly wherever she pleased. She was happy. Aiden stood behind her. A head taller than her, he was a handsome lad with dark hair and azure eyes. His strong arms wrapped tightly around her, his mouth kissing her temple gently. He found something that others were looking for lifetimes. He found true love, the woman of his dreams, a mother to his future children. He was happy and content. She felt the same. Her hand caressed the simple amulet he had given her made from a coin, strung on a leather rope. It was for good luck.

The next scene we saw was a stone-built house. We were approximately in 350 BC in Ireland. Siobhan did not want to go into the house; just feeling this house brought tremendous emotional pain to her. I asked her to show me what happened there. Reluctantly, her soul led us into the house. Siobhan and Aiden were married and lived briefly in this house. Next, we witnessed an argument between Aiden and her. It felt as though Aiden had the urge to participate in a war. It felt like a war against the Roma. His temperament was hot. He was upset that she did not understand that his duty as an Irish Celt was to go with his peers. She was worried. Angrily, he walked out of the house. Tears running down her face, Siobhan stood in her kitchen, gently rubbing her swollen belly. She was about three months pregnant.

As we progressed in the timeline, Siobhan was crying hysterically. Aidan was killed in a battle, and they brought his body home so she could lay him to rest. She ran to the front of the house and saw a simple carriage pulled by two horses. In the back laid the cold dead body of Aiden, covered by a piece of cloth. Her sorrow was inconsolable. They brought the body into the house to be prepared for the funeral. She wanted it like that. She wanted to spend the last few hours with the love of her life before she covered him with soil. The labor pains came fast, and she lost her soul mate and their unborn child that day. She was devastated. She believed it was all her fault. She was angry, blaming herself for everything that had happened. If only she could convince Aiden to stay home that day. If only she had not been so upset. And if only she had not lost their unborn child, she would at least have a part of him with her. She fell into a deep, dark depression and despair. She continued living in the house but secluded herself from everyone. Friends and family would bring her food, hoping she would heal someday.

She refused any company, friendships, and marriage proposals. She lived alone in her sorrow, believing she was the biggest failure. Years passed, and she was healthy but did not care about that. She decided that she didn't deserve to be happy. She wished she could go to sleep and never wake. Someone left paper, paints, and brushes on her doorstep one day. Skeptically, she took them and let them sit in the room. Then, one day, numbed of all feelings, she took the painting supplies into her yard and began painting. Her hand made graceful movements on the paper, to her amazement, as she pained nature like an art prodigy. It felt like someone was standing behind her, holding her tight and guiding each stroke of her hand. Unconditional love was filling her whole being as she painted. She felt like she was again in the arms of her beloved Aiden.

Unfortunately, Siobnah would not share her art with others. She felt ashamed of her life, where she, according to herself, had failed as a wife and mother. She felt embarrassed to be an artist. The time she lived in was not supportive of female artists. Perhaps, if she had had a fire in her soul that truly believed in her art, that she poured her soul into, she would have become successful and respected in her community for it. She lived a long life. She painted many pieces, mainly of nature and birds, but she never shared any of them with others. She died alone and heartbroken with her hand laid over the coin medallion that Aiden had given her when she was young, and they were madly in love.

JAMIE

Jamie (Siobhan) is a Pleiadian starseed that I worked with for a few months to assist her in moving forward. We embarked on each session, the conscious soul-healing journey, through guided meditation (not hypnosis). We let the Pleiadians lead us into the right past lives so we could heal any soul traumas that manifested in her current lifetime as mysterious blockages that were preventing her from having a happy life. Her whole life, Jamie always felt, without any logical explanation, that she had to hide and run from one place to another. When she finished her college studies, she enrolled in another. She was subconsciously delaying the beginning of her real adult life. This is because her soul had the painful memories of losing her soul mate and their unborn child. In addition to these traumas, her secret passion for art brought a lot of inner shame. Her ego manifested all these fantastic opportunities to travel and study. Still, it also suggested thoughts that she was not ready to start her life as a successful artist because the ego's job was to protect her from the same or a similar scenario repeating itself.

This session was different because, in past life sessions, we did not change that particular life's outcome. We only brought unconditional love to the soul for the purpose of soul healing. We understood and accepted the story of that life and healed it with love. This time, the Pleiadians guided Siobhan's soul (in the meditation) to bring all her paintings outside, in her yard, and to invite the village people to come and view them. Her soul needed to overcome her shame of being an artist, as this is her main gift in this lifetime. She has a gift to bring soul healing to others through her artistic expression. Eyes are the doorway to the soul, and art can speak deeply to our soul. Art and the vibrancy of colors brought her soul peace even in that lifetime. All she had to do was forgive herself since those unfortunate events were not her fault. Her soul wanted to heal, and so she did. In our session, she was guided to forgive herself, their unborn child, Aiden, those who killed him, and those who encouraged him to go to war. She filled everyone with unconditional love. She walked into the garden, looking at her paintings. Seeing other people enjoying them, smiling, accepting her the way she was, she was filled with unconditional love. Ultimately, when we left that past life, she surrendered and accepted all that happened. There was nothing more to heal.

When we emerged from mediation, Jamie felt different. She realized she had been running away from her life for fear of being hurt. She told me she was afraid to be in a long-term relationship and was unconsciously self-sabotaging her past relationships.

Her soul remembered how emotionally painful it was. The soul shared this information with her ego at conception. This was so the ego could prevent her from falling in love. The soul was afraid to experience anything like that again. As an added bonus, the ego prevented her from becoming a successful artist, which is her soul calling. According to the soul's information, art would only cause her past negative feelings of shame and failure to awaken, which could lead to self-destructive behavior. See, the ego and soul were functioning based on old programming, making Jamie's life havoc.

After the session, Jamie shared with me that a few weeks before our session, she had reconnected with a man she had known for several years but had not seen in a while. They became romantically involved, and he gave her a golden coin to hold onto. He told her she did not have to keep running away and could do whatever she desired. Now, the future is hers to paint in any colors she chooses, to share with the world.

CHAPTER 3

THE PLEIADIAN MISSION

"Freeing humanity through knowledge." ~ Pleiadians

God created all life in the Universe. The Pleadians, later joined by other star nations, embarked on a research project to learn (in depth) how God works and how God's consciousness works. As part of our journey to understand the magnificence of the Universe, Earth became a significant part shared by us and you since we genetically modified our bodies with Earth's biological components, which later became part of your DNA.

When we first arrived on Earth, we created Lemuria. We could only stay for short periods as our bodies were not in harmony with Earth's atmosphere. We built several Rejuvenation Temples in Lemuria, later in Atlantis, and on the neighboring planets of Maldek and Mars that were easily accessible. We also used Mars as our main intergalactic airport and stored much of our highly advanced technology there. In our spaceships, we would travel back to Pleiades, Sirius, Andromeda, Orion, etc., from Mars. Once home, we would rejuvenate our bodies in our natural environment instead of in the Rejuvenating Temple of Earth. However, that process consumed time and energy quickly.

GENETIC MODIFICATION

Our genetic experiments started in the mid-Atlantean era when our extraterrestrial population grew tremendously due to the increase of other incoming star nations. We had several thriving communities (islands) in Atlantis. Demands for Rejuvenation Temples were growing faster than we could supply. The purpose of the Rejuvenation Temple was to keep our bodies healthy and vibrant. The temple's energy and crystalline grid connected us to the Universal Mind, operating in 5D and higher frequencies.

Let's mentally travel back in time to understand how life on Earth evolved. We begin in Lemuria. There had been very few extraterrestrial scouts visiting Earth before Lemuria. Lemurian civilization was an extraterrestrial civilization with a limited population. We brought many plants, trees, and what you would call magical beings, such as fairies, elves, mermaids, dolphins, dragons, unicorns, etc. It was their wish to be a part of Lemuria. Lemuria was as organic as you could imagine. All extraterrestrial bodies were in deep connection to Universal energy. In continuation, they utilized plant medicine from trees and plants we brought to Earth from our planet. The first plants were from Pleiades.

Beings with more dense bodies used physical energy to create shelters, communities, transportation, and food. Those beings were in greater need of the Rejuvenation Temple. Back then, the effect of rejuvenation lasted for long periods of time, even a hundred years or so.

Lemurians brought on Earth highly advanced technology but utilized it only when needed. They preferred to honor the pristine Earth, live in harmony with the land, follow the laws of nature, and use their intuition and inner guidance connected to God. This civilization was guided primarily by women. You could call them high priestesses, goddesses, or cosmic mothers to awaken your memory. Feminine energy is nourishing, loving, and compassionate. This is how you can describe the energy of Lemuria – nourishing, caring, loving, and full of compassion like a mother's heart. They mastered living from the heart in the third-dimensional world of Earth, staying in their fifth-dimensional soul-mind consciousness. They did not need to build megalithic buildings, use the newest high-tech gadgets, advance materialistically, or change Earth in any way. They honored the Earth and its cornucopia of abundance, natural crystals, pristine nature, and clear waters. Becoming one with the environment helped their bodies adjust slightly more quickly. Their intuition in the Earth realm grew stronger through ceremonies, honoring, and combining the energies of Earth and the Universe. They became true masters of plant medicine, combining Earth's natural resources with those brought from the Universe.

The first DNA genetic manipulation was performed in Lemuria, using plant DNA grown on Earth to merge with extraterrestrial DNA to improve the body. The Plant Kingdom still stores information on ancient Lemurians. This is also why plant medicine is an answer to many physical diseases within the human body. Those who choose to study herbal medicine and essential oils and use their intuition to let plants and trees talk to them are connecting with the ancient Lemurians.

Lemuria was classified as a successful project. Approximately in the third quarter of our time in Lemuria, many other star nations, especially Lyrans, expressed interest in joining us, and we agreed. We knew it would mean expanding our living space, so we explored the inner Earth. Eventually, with our Sirian brothers and sisters, we developed inner cities on Earth that still fully function today.

In this story we are sharing with you, we arrive at the moment of the amazing Atlantean islands full of thriving extraterrestrial communities with overwhelming requests for Rejuvenation Temples because some incoming star nations were thirsty for futuristic life that would mirror their home worlds. When building on Earth, you become a creator in 3D reality, regardless of any higher dimensional cosmic consciousness you may possess. Physical 3D creations do not happen with the power of manifesting through the mind. To physically create, you need to utilize biological materials, of which Earth has an abundance. You have to use tools, which we had, and you have to use physical power. No matter how sophisticated the tools are, you still need to use physical strength to create, even if it is to just push the buttons. We did much more than push the buttons. We are explaining this clearly so you can relate to us and our experiences. Our bodies, in Atlantis, were not good at performing physical tasks and were constantly becoming increasingly ill from the atmosphere. Thus, we needed to come to the Rejuvenation Temple often, much more often than in Lemurian times. We thought every 10 years was too frequent, but it decreased to once yearly. That was dramatic since our natural life span was several thousands of years.

Lyrans suggested using genetic engineering to alter our extraterrestrial bodies with DNA from the Animal Kingdom to help solve health issues. They already had experience with it after launching successful genetic modifications and DNA merging projects in Centaurus. All twelve original star nations' representatives saw it as a beneficial adjustment and unanimously agreed to proceed.

The original agreement was to use animal DNA since plant DNA was not working as efficiently as we needed to sustain our desired physical body. We used various animal DNA but did not use primates' DNA for this project. It was meant to be a controlled experiment and only used for our star races.

Looking back, seeing the failure, there is no need to point fingers at Pleiadians, Sirians, Lyrans, or any other singular star nation. We had all agreed to it. We all share responsibility for the later transformation of primate DNA into human DNA because we collectively enabled this technology to be used on Earth, even though it was meant only for us to use initially.

To understand this better, our actions of genetically modified bodies were based on the similar endeavor you are trying to achieve today, to be able to live on Mars. If you had the knowledge, you would genetically modify your body to thrive on Mars for extended periods while staying connected to your families on Earth. We were like you today, just a little more advanced.

Spiritual and Mathematical Codes

How did we do it? We followed spiritual and mathematical codes associated with how the Universe was created. In other words, we followed the laws of nature and the Universe. Remember that the Lemurian extraterrestrial civilization thrived spiritually, and the Atlantean extraterrestrial civilization thrived technologically. After living together for an extended period, we amalgamated and applied elements from both.

Earth is known as a place of duality. It thrives in the "give and take" (action-reaction) pattern. Since we wanted to embody this avatar (body), we had to become one with the Earthly body and "give." Our contribution to Earth was our extraterrestrial DNA, which contains our cosmic knowledge.

SURROGATE GOD CRYSTAL

When we first started combining animal DNA (we will call this physical DNA) and our extraterrestrial DNA (we will call this cosmic DNA), we were unsuccessful in keeping the soul thriving in the genetically modified body. The soul's energy naturally gravitated toward the higher realms, our home in that lifetime. It's the same as a boat's sail on the ocean; the soul sails in the divine energy with its compass set to return home. Naturally, the soul wanted to be free of the body heavied by low vibrational animal consciousness (animal DNA) even though animal DNA made the body healthier. Therefore, we had to lock it in, like how you would keep a bird in a cage to prevent it from flying away.

Our genetic engineers devised a spectacular idea to create a Surrogate God simulator within the Mineral Kingdom to temporarily confuse the soul's energy into thinking it belongs with the animals on Earth. This would work since the newly modified body shared the animal's DNA, and instead of gravitating toward the real God's energy, the soul felt falsely comfortable with the Surrogate God. As you would build a server that controls numerous computers, we conditioned Earth's crystal to hold this combined DNA to control all the souls on Earth. We played God and created a God-like simulator (a powerful magnet for the soul) so the soul would thrive in the physical body instead of wanting to "fly away." We willingly anchored, trapped, and imprisoned our soul essence on Earth.

The Surrogate God crystal became our DNA's central repository.

As an unexpected bonus, we realized that when the body malfunctions (dies) and the soul leaves, the soul could quickly return to the Earth realm after leaving the body. We were thrilled upon this discovery. Our anchor truly worked. This opened such incredible opportunities for us to live on Earth for extended periods of time while experiencing different bodies. After each birth, we experienced "consciousness amnesia." However, we knew how to correct it after the birth. Most star beings loved residing on Earth. It was meant to be a paradise for our star brothers and sisters to visit. As time passed, we stopped worrying that we dramatically altered our evolution. After all, it was only meant to be a temporary fix until we were ready to return home.

Later, the Annunaki used the same technology to speed up the evolution of natural primates and created human beings. (We will share more about this later.)

Initially, we thought the DNA alternation could be reversed by removing the anchor from the Surrogate God Crystal, like deleting a file in your computer. Unfortunately, it became more complicated than that. We jumped on this genetic modification project without any prior trials on Earth. Not fully aware of how animal DNA would alter our consciousness, most of us fully participated without questions. As time passed, numerous star beings started to experience unwanted side effects of the Earth's animal low-vibration energy, and we learned about the ego. The ego, in other words, defines animal DNA. We began to experience feelings such as greed, pride, fear, hate, guilt, shame, etc. Some started to act based on these emotions. We called them ego-possessed beings; throughout history, they have been called Sons of Belial and are on the Path of Dark. Those who managed to stay on a spiritual Path of Light are known in your history as the Children of the Law of One.

It's important to remember that initially, everyone had good intentions, but things spiraled out of control. We merged the 5D soul-mind consciousness with the 3D consciousness of the animal ego, and we eventually became stuck on Earth. Earth is physically 3D, and 3D energy is much denser than the 5D (or higher) energy from which we operate.

Many star beings became obsessed with their new, highly functioning bodies. The technology was magnificent, and Earth's resources were plentiful. They paid less and less attention to their soul and their spiritual energy. The animal ego literally possessed them. You know the saying that you cannot help those who do not want to be helped. It is as accurate today as it was in Atlantis.

In summary, twelve star nations anchored their cosmic consciousness in the Mineral Kingdom of the Earth and utilized the Earth's crystal to hold this knowledge. If you entertain the possibility that Earth is running like a computer program, then the metaphor will be that we have put our memory chip in the crystal, which is the main part of your motherboard. Our energy is still there.

STAR MAP

Body is a microcosm of macrocosm. The star map is left within the physical body as an artist leaves a signature in their painting. The Earth was one of twelve planets in your solar system. A human being has twelve strands of DNA and twelve main meridians. There is one more DNA strand, the 13th strand. We call this strand a God's line. It functions through the central nervous system; it fuses all twelve strands and is, in a way, invisible. The human DNA code is 12+1. The 13th strand is the light of all creation (light of God) within. We (extraterrestrials included) all have the 13th strand, regardless of how we look, who we are, or where we live in our Universe. Thus, we are all God, and God is us.

STAR MAP IN CHAKRAS

The physical body has seven main chakras because the Earth was the seventh planet from the outer ring. Chakras are your horizontal energy. Each chakra is like a separate planet and has a ring around it. Each chakra is also a floor filled with books of life, or in other words, your personal Akashic library filled with knowledge from each life you have experienced. Each ring creates a layer of your aura, also known as your electromagnetic field, that magnetizes your reality.

In many creation stories, the Seven Pleiadian Sisters are mentioned. If you gaze at the stars, you can identify seven Pleiadian planets, even though there are a few more. These seven planets are considered the most significant. Additionally, there are seven days a week, seven continents on Earth, seven colors in the rainbow, and ancient stories about rainbow bodies. Is it just a coincidence that the number seven is so prevalent?

The seven main chakras could be better understood when split into three groups. Each group has a particular purpose in your evolution.

Group number 1 is the base chakra, sacral chakra, and solar plexus. These three chakras are nourished by the red color healing ray. They store the energy information from past and past lives on Earth. They are deeply connected to Earth's physical energy (Mineral Kingdom, Plant Kingdom, and Animal Kingdom).

Group number 2 is the heart chakra, a seat for the soul nourished by the green color healing ray. It is connected to your higher self, cosmic consciousness, soul family, the Universal Mind, and the future.

Group number 3 is the throat, brow, and crown chakras. The blue healing ray nourishes these three chakras.

They have nothing to do with the past or the future; their hidden energy is the power of now and the creation of your reality. These three chakras deeply influence the nervous system. The electromagnetic nervous system co-creates your reality based on your thoughts and feelings. You are the creator of your life.

Now, let's play with a little metaphor. Your heart is your Sun that energizes your solar battery. It is the center of your Universe (your body). Like Earth orbits around the Sun, these chakras orbit your heart. Some are connected on the same orbit line (3rd and 5th chakra, 2nd and 6th chakra, 1st and 7th chakra). This means they share similar/compatible energy. Numerologically looking, each of these connections is equal to the number 8. The spiritual meaning of the number eight is pointing to your infinity and knowledge that you are made in the image of God.

$$3+5=8$$
$$2+6=8$$
$$1+7=8$$

To share more understanding of chakras, individual seven chakras are dominated by either the ego's or soul's energy. (When the ego evolves, it matures into the mind, dominating the chakras in harmony with the soul.) These two energies are two main DNA strands: the cosmic/spiritual (soul) and the physical (ego). Now, remember the part when we spoke about needing to create the Surrogate God's energy to anchor our soul within the core of the Earth? We had to install light codes into the physical energy. We paid attention to all the details.

First Chakra – Physical (ego)
Mother/Father – Surrogate God particle – You wanted to come down to Earth; we gave you survival skills.
Second Chakra – Cosmic/spiritual (soul)

You—the original energy of your blueprint—have childhood innocence, happy emotions, and creativity. The original energy has no fear of anyone harming you or you fulfilling any responsibilities (like paying bills). It has no survival skills, such as getting food or finding shelter. The energy is pure, innocent, happy, and loving.

Third Chakra – Physical (ego)

Mother/Father – Surrogate God particle – When you mature in Earth years, you can take care of your own survival. You can build toward the survival of other generations and keep the reincarnating cycle repeating. Fear ensures survival.

Fourth Chakra – Cosmic/spiritual (soul)

You – the original energy of your blueprint - Love heals all wounds. Acceptance, unconditional love, compassion, and forgiveness heal are natural parts of your original blueprint energy. Unconditional love is the highest energy in this Universe. Love is the soul's healing light code that your soul will never forget. That is why everyone needs love, unconditional cosmic love.

Fifth Chakra – Physical (ego)

Mother/Father—Surrogate God particle—We gave you a voice to speak your needs (sound frequency), express yourself, and create the reality YOU want to experience in the physical world. We left the true God's particle (not surrogate) within for you to be a creator of your own reality.

Sixth Chakra – Cosmic/spiritual (soul)

You – your blueprint's original energy- is the connection to your higher self, to your cosmic consciousness. When you shift from an unhappy mind to a happy mind, your higher self will share guidance, ideas, inspiration, and knowledge so that you can free your soul from entrapment in the body and will function from the same body in an uplifting, peaceful, creative way.

Seventh Chakra – Physical (ego)

Mother/Father – Surrogate God particle – We kept the connection with you for all the time you spent on Earth. Trust is the key to opening the door from physical ego-mind amnesia into the divine kingdom of God and communion with your soul family.

STAR MAP IN MERIDIANS

According to Chinese medicine, your body has twelve main vertical energy lines called meridians. These meridians are interconnected, forming a meridian wheel. Each meridian carries energy to and from at least one physical organ, maintaining healthy blood circulation and a strong immune system.

The body has many meridians. You only need to know two more and the mentioned twelve to understand their connection to DNA. They are - central and governing meridians. Their energy pathways can form one circuit that connects the front and back of the body, represented by the Ouroboros symbol. These meridians supply energy to the nervous system from all organs and all seven chakras. They are responsible for your innate energy and could influence the pineal gland (vertical energy) and thymus (horizontal energy), essential in your healing and evolution.

When central and governing meridians form one circuit, they become the 13th meridian pathway that we call God's line (+1). Once again, your DNA code is 12+1. Each of the twelve meridians contains information from one DNA strand corresponding to ten organs: blood, immunity, and (+1) nervous systems.

For now, we will focus on twelve main meridians. Six are dominated by the Earth's energy, influencing physical DNA. Those are - the small intestines, kidney, triple warmer (immunity system), liver, large intestines, and spleen.

The other six are dominated by Cosmic energy and influence cosmic DNA. They are the heart, bladder, circulation, gallbladder, lung, and stomach.

This information will help you when practicing energy healing. Earth's meridians need more Earth's energy, while Cosmic meridians need more Cosmic energy.

Twelve meridians can be identified by color or number, like chakras. We will give you the color code, slightly different from what you are used to for these organs. Notice that Earth DNA meridians overlap in each color code, but Cosmic DNA meridians are only one per color code. You can use these colors to heal organs, as mentioned below.

Red – triple warmer (immunity system), gallbladder, liver
Orange – liver, lungs, large intestines
Yellow – large intestines, stomach, spleen
Green – spleen, heart, small intestines
Blue – light and dark blue – small intestines, bladder, kidney
Violet – kidney, circulation (blood), triple warmer (immunity system)

The core aspect of ancient Atlantean healing (Soul Healing) is healing in the combination of chakras, meridians, and God's line (nervous system). It is much more complex than what we have shared. We are sharing those relevant parts to awaken your knowledge of who you are. We desire to share information that will trigger memories of your ancient DNA that will spontaneously activate your DNA if this is your soul's wish. You can also set intentions right now to connect to the healing energy for your soul, mind, and body.

SPIRAL STAR MAP IN GOD'S LINE (NERVOUS SYSTEM) - LANGUAGE OF NUMBERS AND SPIRITUAL MEANING OF FIBONACCI SEQUENCE

It is believed that God's language, the universal Language of Light, can be expressed through numbers. If this is true, these numbers are linked to God's line and your 13th strand of DNA. Furthermore, numbers can be expressed through frequency, impacting the nervous system.

Human beings can possess extraordinary abilities determined by the strength of their nervous system, specifically the nervous system's electromagnetic frequency (EM) and the synchronization of their heart-mind coherence. Since EM waves are a type of light wave, they carry a frequency that is a part of God's Language of Light. All abilities considered superhuman can be developed through the proper knowledge and discipline. Therefore, these abilities are trainable and can be learned by anyone who is determined to do so.

The language of numbers could be visually represented in geometric patterns frequently seen in nature, art, architecture, and even in the human body using the Golden Ratio mathematical formula, closely linked with the Fibonacci sequence. This sequence of numbers exhibits a unique property where each number is the sum of the two preceding numbers. 0, 1, 1, 2, 3, 5, 8, 13, 21, etc. Since Earth is a place of duality, everything has two explanations: physical (ego's intellectual version) and spiritual (soul's cosmic version), the Fibonacci sequence includes. This knowledge used to be taught in mystery schools.

WEAVING YOUR DESTINY - WORKING WITH SPIRITUAL MEANING OF FIBONACCI SEQUENCE AND CHAKRAS

Think of the Fibonacci sequence as a spiraled road to enlightenment and return home. In spiritual meaning, this journey has eight major stops correlating with your chakras - stories of your lives (the main focus/action of this book), resulting in the reaction - of healing - your twelve meridians pathways (ten organs, blood, immune system) and strengthening/repairing the nervous system. The number eight signifies infinity, pointing to infinite YOU and your infinite choices. Since number zero means nothing, you will start your journey at number 1, then continue in sequence 1, 2, 3, 5, 8, 13, and have the last stop at 21. Each step has signature wisdom teaching and frequency, and once you master it, you can move forward. You will face three trap doors and often spiral backward during your journey. That is normal; it's like playing a game, so don't worry and become a great player. When backspiral happens, evaluate, correct, and move forward. This teaching is not meant to be a race but a roadmap to an enjoyable way of life. Here is the condensed version.

First Stop
Number 1 – 4th Chakra – The spiritual awakening of the spiritual Fibonacci sequence of your star-seeded being starts at the center of your own Universe – your heart – the fourth chakra, which is the seat of your soul. It is a cosmic/spiritual, soul-dominated chakra. Interestingly enough, the heart is the first organ created in the embryo.

When you go through your life without any spiritual awakening, the spiritual Fibonacci sequence has no meaning to you. You could have a good life, according to your own requirement of what a good life is, whatever makes you happy. This is totally acceptable.

The activation of the spiritual Fibonacci sequence and awakening of the fourth chakra often occur as a result of a shocking trigger in your life. For example, illness, accidents, abuse, tremendous suffering, tragedy, etc. Unfortunately, happy events do not trigger this energy of transformation, except for a few exceptions, because when you are happy, content, or in love, making life-altering spiritual changes is not a priority. It is also important to mention that no one is responsible for the misery in your life; your soul planned this awakening around 400 years ago.

Awakening in the fourth chakra shocks the body, temporarily enlivening your cosmic consciousness, often resulting in incredible feelings experienced throughout the body or an unforgettable mystical experience. It's like you were given instant temporary access to extraordinary hearing, feeling, seeing, tasting, and smelling the truth. All your senses are fully active, and you may experience superhuman abilities or miraculous healing. As you become more aware of your infinite soul, you will consciously experience positive energy, love, and happiness that you may have never felt before, and you will experience spiritual highs. Arriving consciously into the heart is a life-changing experience. To sustain this energy, you need to take new actions. Learning to be conscious and present is essential. This means being aware and focused on the present moment. You have been looking at your life with a positive bias, dwelling on the past while trying to make it seem better than it was. You will realize that you have been dwelling on the past while trying to make it seem better than it was. At this point, your life needs to be re-evaluated. See what is working or what is not working for you. Ask yourself this question, "Where will I go from here?"

You will slowly start losing the "I" identity - your old identity. You may feel sad, lost, and confused for a while. This is a good time to work with the energy of forgiveness for yourself and others. Be gentle with yourself. Love yourself for who you are instead of what others want you to be. Learn to understand yourself. One day, you will wake up feeling the energy of your inner power, your true soul power. This is a little tease, but it feels incredible because it is your soul power, not your altered ego. It is like your inner GPS has activated on your life mission. You must practice quieting your thinking mind (ego) to feel your inner GPS. Follow your passion and joy and start creating from the heart.

Second Stop

Number 1 – 3rd Chakra – From the heart chakra, the spiral will go down to your third chakra in a clockwise motion. The third chakra is the seat of the ego. In the embryo, the gallbladder is the second organ that emerges. (Modern science recognizes the liver as the second organ created in the human body.)The energy of the ego affects the gallbladder and liver, which can hold physical emotions like anger, hate, jealousy, rejection, fear, etc., greatly affecting your thinking choices.

Upon awakening in the heart chakra, your ego may sense that trouble is on the horizon. This is because the ego's primary function is to ensure your survival and possible reproduction. The ego also tends to create negative feelings and emotions, such as self-victimization or bullying, to remind you of how stuck you are in your life. Regardless of your financial or physical health, the ego loves to cause suffering and pretend to be your hero by saving you from it every time.

When you start to work with your ego, you can view it as your scared pet that needs lots of love. You can give it a name, converse, and laugh together about its silly, unhappy actions. Work with the energy of acceptance; accept everything that has happened. Notice when you feel like a victim or when you feel like a bully. Do not judge yourself or others; become a reasonable observer. Become conscious of your physical actions and behavior. Remember that the third chakra is physical energy, ego-dominated energy. Later in this book, you will learn how to heal and harmonize the victim and the bully's energy.

Third Stop
Number 2 – (1+1=2) 4th and 3rd Chakra - This is the first time two chakras connect to form an energy circuit and interact. The energy fourth chakra (your soul) and the third chakra (your ego) enter a dance of duality, creating a conscious circle. It is a push-pull energy. You have spiritual highs and physical lows. This energy is your first trap door, as it challenges you. In mystery schools, challenges were part of the curriculum. In your current life, a majority of you do not have time to spend a few years of proper training in the mystery school. So, according to your soul contract for this life, the mystery school is woven into your everyday life, with tests as well.

When you open the first trap door, you are flooded with energies of shame and guilt from your past. You are feeling it emotionally and physically. Even if you awaken to spirituality, you can still be stuck here for a lifetime. Working through feelings of shame and guilt is key to healing. Ask questions like - Why do you feel like that? What are you afraid of? Who do you blame for what happened to you in the past? Acceptance, forgiveness, and self-love will help you heal and pass this trap door.

Energy Exercise:

Put your left hand on your solar plexus and your right hand on your heart chakra. Close your eyes and focus on your breath. Continue until you feel your breathing slow down.

Imagine walking inside your heart (your soul), walking down into your solar plexus (your ego). Meet your ego. You may imagine your ego any way you like, a pet, another part of yourself, or anything that helps you to connect with it. Talk to your ego, have a good conversation with yourself, ask what upsets you, what scares you, and so on. Pick one issue at a time. Still keeping your left hand over your solar plexus and your right hand over your heart, discuss it with your ego. Ask if both of you can accept it. When you reach acceptance, bring this "issue" into the heart. Forgive yourself as well as everyone else involved in this "issue." Learn to become best friends with your soul and with your ego. That is self-love.

Fourth Stop

Number 3 – (2+1=3) 5th Chakra – In a clockwise motion, follow the spiritual Fibonacci spiral from the third chakra into the fifth chakra. Please do not focus on the visual ratio proportions but instead, follow the number sequence here:

(4th chakra + 3rdchakra) + 5thchakra or (1+1)+1=2+1=3

Number 3 is a catalyst; you will work with two physical chakras and one cosmic/spiritual chakra. Therefore, manifestation in your physical reality is predominant here. This stimulates the nervous system (your frequency), which is interconnected with all bodily functions and chakras, allowing you to change your life patterns and reality, as well as your physical circumstances and reality.

If you wish to change your life, you must alter your way of expressing yourself—the way you think and the way you speak. This will change your frequency and attract the desired circumstances in your new reality.

This will also trigger various types of fears or anger. Experiencing these symptoms is normal; if you are, congratulate yourself because it means you are on the right track! You will be working on healing your fears of being seen and heard and reaching the first level of opportunity to reprogram your energy. Anger is just another form of fear. Acceptance, forgiveness, and unconditional love are the trinity of energy that can create a powerful catalyst in your life if they become your way of life, and you can explore new resonating frequencies. For example, You may have a preprogrammed frequency keeping you in poverty (pre-birth soul contract). You will have the chance to consciously switch to a frequency of abundance. What does abundance mean to you? How does it feel? What do you need to let go (accept, forgive, love unconditionally) to become a regular part of your life?

When you start expressing yourself in a positive frequency, no matter what happens to you, good or bad, it will become a new way of life for you. You will embrace the good and understand that everything bad happens for a reason. This positive way of thinking will open doors to synchronicity in your life. You will start noticing more guidance and help, which has always been present, but you couldn't perceive it as prominently as before. You will manifest what you desire in a short period. This is a beautiful place to be.

Fifth Stop
Number 5 – (3+2=5) 1st Chakra - in a clockwise motion, you will travel down from the 5th chakra to arrive at the 1st chakra, the energy of physical survival. You will work with three physical chakras and two cosmic/spiritual chakras.

(5th chakra + 4th chakra + 3rd chakra) + (2nd chakra + 1st chakra) = 5, or 3+2=5

When you reach this energy level, you will likely be on your spiritual journey for a while, maybe even many years. You may question your incarnations and want to return home to the Universe. You will be challenged with another level of fear, shame, and guilt. You shed and heal these energies in several layers, like peeling an onion.

This energy puts you on the doorstep of the second trap door. Your soul wants you to pass this second trap door, while your ego fears for your physical survival more than ever. It would do anything to keep you here, even making you sick or manifesting all kinds of chaos to keep you stuck here. Your human ego enables you to be spiritual and grow to impressive degrees of awareness. However, its program is to keep you safe and alive. Walking beyond this point is unknown territory for the ego. Imagine your ego as your pet dog, who is scared and barking loudly.

Once again, you have to face your fears. At this time, those fears are combined in one "fear monster" that the ego lovingly created to protect you. It is essential to understand your ego energy to forgive yourself. You are part of that ego, as that ego is part of you. Forgiveness, unconditional love, and divine light to illuminate your future path are the trinity for the catalyst you need here.

Conscious healing of your past lives is essential at this level. You will begin to heal your multiple lifetimes of PTSD while healing soul wounds that keep you a prisoner in the incarnation cycle.

Walking through this passage is like walking through a dark tunnel. You cannot see the light on the other side for much of this walk. It is not fun. Once you start seeing the light and feeling God's divine guidance, you can reprogram your 3D survival mode to the higher consciousness (5D thriving mode) while staying in the physical body. This is the point when you are consciously starting to connect with the 4D and 5D energy like your ancestors did. You will no longer accidentally tap into this energy; you will embody this energy instead.

Love is the most important and key frequency that you will need to pass this level. When one has a love for someone or something (more than with itself), one is capable of doing unbelievable things. One in love is in a flow of a miraculous frequency where everything is possible. The progression happens from fear to love to peace. The love frequency is the best way. Do not be afraid to feel emotions with your human heart.

Sixth Stop

Number 8 – (5+3=8) – The 8th step from your first chakra is your energy point above your head.

(1st chakra +2nd chakra +3rd chakra +4th chakra +5th chakra) + (6th chakra +7th chakra + 8th point) = 8 or 5+3=8

Number eight holds the energy of divine intervention to remind you of your infinity, but it will also test you. This is your third trap door. In ordinary life, this is an energy level where your soul transitions from the physical body into Heaven after you pass away. However, when you consciously reach this energy while still in your physical body, you are consciously connected to the 4D energies. You may be astral traveling, connecting to other dimensions, or experimenting with parallel lives. This is fun, but be aware of your experience. You may get lost in these places, and it can manifest as a mental illness in your body. This is why we discourage you from using any hallucinogens, drugs, alcohol, or teaching plants to stimulate your mind. Learn to work with this energy level with a clear, conscious mind. Learn to discern the energy. You do not want to propel yourself unprepared into this energy level for any fraction of time. As exciting as it may sound, it is not worth it.

This energy level has all kinds of negative energy attached to it, which only wants to possess the body. Spirit attachments and possessions are because they intensely desire to be in the body, so they will shamelessly attach to anyone willing to host them (invite them in).

Even these entities and energies must follow the free will law, so they will impose as teachers, guides, angels, and descended family spirits. They want to trick you into inviting them using your free will so that they can enter your energy field and ultimately live through your body. They will figure out your weaknesses. They will be whatever you subconsciously want them to be. They may temporarily help or share some amazing information with you. However, they eventually will devastatingly gain control of your life, living through you. You should learn how to test the energy. You can use kinesiology testing, such as the body pendulum technique (asking yes/no answer questions). Ask questions three times, for example, "Are you coming from the love and light?" Receiving a "yes" answer three times in a row will show positive energy. Negative energy cannot lie three times in a row. This will help you to distinguish between positive and negative energies. Before asking questions, determine the yes/no position. Calibrate yourself to receive the truth by stating three times, "I am calibrating myself to the truth," and receiving three times, yes.

This energy level will also challenge your ego, which will always be a part of you while you are still in the physical body. At this point, sadly, many spiritual workers develop a spiritual ego and start seeing themselves as better than others. They know more, have seen it all, and may have been told they are the incarnation of some significant figure in your history. Stay away from getting stuck here; it is simply a trap door! You may develop some impressive abilities, have a gift of healing, and be in service to humanity. However, there are still a few steps ahead of you to reach enlightenment while still in your body.

If some of you decide to stay at this level, we lovingly respect that. We know that you will have to face the fear of death to cross this rite of passage, most likely several times. You will face survival-based fears, yet this may be the most exciting part of your life.

The number eight is about infinity, building trust with the Universe and God, defining what word God means to you, and what kind of frequency you create for this word. It is an important word, so do not dismiss it.

To walk through the trap door at this energy level, you will master how to discern energy. You will build trust with your heart's guidance, feel unconditional love from God, and know you are not alone. You will know that everything happens for a reason and that you will be okay. You are just experiencing earthquakes in your life (on various scales); however, if you are ready to let go and let God, you will truly step into the shoes of a humanitarian, a light worker, and the true teacher that you are. Restoring your trust in God is a key component here. Before moving to the next stop, you must heal your soul-mind consciousness. What happened on Earth has to be healed on Earth through the physical human body.

Seventh Stop
Number 13 – (8+5=13) - Continuing clockwise, count another 13 steps down, and you will reach the beginning, the Surrogate God crystal.

While retrieving your soul-mind consciousness from the crystal, you will understand all lower energy and its purpose. You will be connected to the Animal, Plant, and Mineral Kingdoms. You will begin to consciously work on detachment from everyone and everything. At this point, your intuition and trust in God will be solid. You will be guided on your journey. Your body will undergo purification, your soul-mind will be fully healed, and you will have full knowledge of your past. Completion of your soul healing is a key component here.

Eight Stop

Number 21 – (13+8=21) - This will be your last transition level and full embodiment of 5D energy. You will journey through your life (past, present, and future) without any effects of your animal DNA (your ego) because the ego will become an intelligent mind. Even though you may be in the human body (you need to be in the physical body to completely master unplugging from the grid), you will no longer be interested in human life, such as earning a living, having a house, going on vacations, eating food, etc. You will seek solitude in nature as nature soothes your soul. If you find others like you on the same path at the same level, you may be drawn to spend the rest of your life living together as the ancient Lemurians did, in harmony with nature.

If you reach this level, share this with humanity by creating from your God's consciousness. If you leave books or megalithic structures, etc., made from this energy level, they will be here for a long time but will not bind you to this realm anymore. However, creating will be challenging as you will have no need, but we encourage you to create and, for that reason, consciously return back to the sixth stop. You will know how to return here at your will at any time. You will fully embrace "Being God." You will be guided by God's consciousness on what to create, and that will leave a starry trail behind you so that others can find their way back home.

Finding peace within is the key to preventing spontaneous, unwanted backspiraling. The three essentials are understanding and trusting God's consciousness, Cosmic consciousness, and yourself. You can stay on this step as long as you wish to, while still in the physical body, until you are ready to go back home, consciously, by your own free will.

THE GAME OF LIFE

Imagine that life on Earth is like a simulation from a video game, and you have your game set on eight levels. You need to watch out for three trap doors. The goal is to grab the crystal and get to the eighth stop. You can repeat the whole game or willingly go home and start a new game where the setting is not on Earth.

CHAPTER 4

GOD IS A TRIANGLE

"God is a triangle, and so are you." ~ Pleiadians

Sometimes, you may look at a simple object like a triangle and be skeptical of its spiritual significance. After all, it's just a shape with three corners, which can be measured and defined mathematically. However, you must look beyond its physical properties and understand its spiritual meaning and what it means to your physical and spiritual selves. A simple triangle can define God; since we all have been created by God's consciousness, it can define us. How can you benefit from this knowledge? To become one with God, you must identify the three aspects of yourself that correspond to the three parts of a triangle.

The ancient Greek mathematician Pythagoras introduced his students to this formula to calculate the sides of a triangle.

$$a^2 + b^2 = c^2$$

Numbers are a universal language. They are a part of the Language of Light that our ancient ancestors understood and spoke. The Tower of Babel's fall marks a time when the universal language was intentionally confused, scrambled, and separated into many different languages so humans could not freely communicate. They could no longer share the knowledge they had. Languages you speak today are composed of letters or symbols, not numbers or geometric shapes. Therefore, numbers and geometric shapes are a part of the original language that cannot be scrambled. God designed this Universe with mathematical precision, and no one has the power to override the code of God. If geometric shapes could speak their whole meaning audibly, you would have all the answers you seek.

As we mentioned earlier, Earth is a place of duality. Everything has a physical and a spiritual component. Even numbers do. The physical part of a number represents logical precision and explanation. In this part, there is no room for mistakes. The spiritual part of a number represents knowledge, wisdom, guidance, evolution, and room for growth, and when there is room for growth, there is also a space for mistakes. Some of these mistakes turn out to be the latest inventions for humankind. However, it is essential to remember that everything happens in a well-defined and controlled space of numbers and shapes. There is no such thing as a coincidence. Everything happens for a reason.

Let's look at Pythagoras's formula and apply spiritual definition to it.

a = to your EGO (survival ruled by fear)
b = to your SOUL (knowledge)
c = to the conscious YOU (creator)

Next, we need each subject to be in the power of two. In a spiritual meaning, the number two represents duality and choices. In a geometric shape, duality is expressed in a circle. In this formula, we use two opposite qualities that amplify each other and create destructive life patterns based on fear. This is a destructive 3D creator program with a survival program of the ego. When harmonized, these two parts will create a balanced union, and you will manifest a creative 5D creator program with a thriving program of the mind. This is similar to the symbol of dark and light in a circle, where neutral energy, the (perfect middle), is the outcome.

The two parts:
EGO = victim, bully
SOUL = soul wounds (blockages from the past, S-PTSD), worries over the future
YOU = creative, destructive

The ego splits between victim and bully. Your physical DNA is defined in your human ego and operates from that energy level. The ego, depending on your childhood, shapes you either into a victim or a bully. This usually happens between the ages of 7-14, as this is your first set of "ego-influenced" years. Remember, the ego's main job is to secure your survival and possible reproduction. Based on your early childhood circumstances, your ego will install a main program to ensure your survival. There are only two programs to choose from – victim or bully. One of them becomes the main program, but you can quickly fluctuate between both personalities depending on your current physical life challenges.

On a side note, do not get your feathers ruffled by the words victim or bully. These are just words to describe physical energies. Your job is to fully understand their meaning and how they control you. If you have already worked through these energies, your ego is neutral, and the sound of these words will not rattle your nerves.

In reality, the soul is always whole. However, its function in 3D reality has two aspects: the part that is blocked and needs healing and the part that worries about the future choices you will make because you are too wounded to listen to your soul's guidance. Your soul speaks in the language of love. Can you hear it?

Since you anchored part of your soul in the crystal, you are trapped in repeating the reincarnation pattern. Each incarnation brings challenges and could leave significant emotional wounds on your soul. The only way to exit the incarnation cycle and disconnect from the crystal is to gain spiritual knowledge and heal all your soul wounds. Your soul healing must be done from the physical body while living on Earth. As we have said before, what happened on Earth has to be healed on Earth. You will have neutral soul energy once your soul is healed from all current and past lives, and you will stop worrying about the future.

Your personal energy splits between creative and destructive energy. Your power (all your knowledge) is stored in your soul, not your ego, because your ego would misuse it, even with good intentions. You will become god-like and fully unlock your extraterrestrial knowledge and abilities when you heal all parts of your being.

If you look back into your ancient history, you have documented many stories of gods (extraterrestrials) who were creative and destructive. As a god, you also have the power of creativity and destruction that can be used to create amazing things or possibly destroy all of humanity. We do not have to go too far back to remind you of nuclear bombs. The question is, are you ready to be YOU? Are you prepared to take responsibility for knowing without taking advantage of your skills and knowledge? Can you stay humble? Can you hold the frequency of unconditional love? Can you be a father or a mother to all who need it? Can you become a true teacher to seekers? Can you bear the pain of humanity on your shoulders yet understand that you can only help those who are genuinely ready for a transformation? Could you accept that you are not the judge and shall not take the destiny of others into your own hands unless they agree one hundred percent, within their soul, on the action taken? If you answer yes to all these questions, you shall achieve your goal.

When you become a true teacher, a new human, and a god-like, you will clearly see what is dysfunctional and know how to help. It may be through technology, inventions, healing, counseling, or just by holding the frequency of quiet peace and unconditional love, depending on your calling. Nevertheless, you must respect if someone chooses a path of suffering for whatever reason. Everyone's free choice is to choose a path of suffering or happiness. When you reach the point of becoming god, you have chosen the path of happiness and are leaving a golden path behind you for others to follow when they are ready. You can offer a helping hand but let others walk the path for themselves.

When you understand these words, we will apply them to the formula:

$$a^2 + b^2 = c^2$$

EGO (powered by the victim/bully energies) + SOUL (powered by soul wounds/soul worries) = YOU (powered by your creative/destructive power energies - fire)

The ego and soul are programmed to stimulate your reality because suffering aids in faster evolution. YOU are the variable, the catalyst to change your life or stay where you are. You can be anything you would like to be!

THE AWARENESS FACTOR

The triangle equation is the awareness factor. It activates the memory of the Language of Light within your consciousness. The process of changes starts before you even start looking at the formula. This is because it began the moment you became aware of it. In the language of numbers, awareness is represented by the number three. Number one represents a new beginning or a single choice. Number two represents duality, two choices. The third number will give you awareness of the past, present, and future. It gives you three choices (think of fairytales with three wishes), giving you the power to create in the physical realm.

Awareness is a triangle. You start out in awareness to find your true self. When you are aware, you are more likely to be neutral, choose healing, have a good life, kindle your creative fire, etc. Working with this equation will assist you in re-programing and re-patterning your life so that you can have a life filled with love and happiness.

For now, we will leave you with this theory. In the following chapters, you will learn how to work with your ego to achieve neutral energy. You will also learn about your major soul wounds and how to heal them. It is your choice to let go of the fear of the future. We are by your side.

CHAPTER 5

PHYSICAL DNA

We, the Pleiadians, always marvel over human creation. You think you are so complicated and often make matters more complex than need be. At times, you feel that no one understands, no one loves you, and everyone has deserted you, or you rise into your warrior self and are ready to take on the whole world, all by yourself, like a stubborn mule.

You are never alone. We invite you to work in union with us and feel equal. We would like you to simplify all the information you have. This is one reason this book is written in straightforward terms that everyone can understand. We intend you to understand the emotions that keep you stuck. We are assisting you in freeing you from your human slavery by giving you knowledge instead of physically interfering in your reality. We may keep repeating ourselves so that you might have an "aha" moment in which you will have all the necessary information to change your life. You are your own healer! You are your own guru! It is the knowledge that will break your invisible chains. It is unconditional love that will help you heal. You need to become an active part of your physical and spiritual healing.

The following two chapters will focus on physical DNA. Firstly, you will receive a theory with examples and practical tools for your transformation. It may sound boring, but this practical knowledge has always existed on Earth. All true teachers in the ancient past (and present) utilize these tools, although they may just call them different names.

It is important to understand that the ego is a side effect of the animal DNA—physical DNA—that has been used to create the physical body. The ego's energy is very different from the soul energy (spiritual energy) that came from benevolent extraterrestrials.

BASIC FUNCTION

The ego operates only on low-dimensional energy, as it knows nothing else. As mentioned earlier, the ego's job is to ensure your survival and possible reproduction. Its energy has been there with you since conception. For the first nine months of your life in your mother's womb, the ego exchanged files with the soul and observed your family dynamics. This is so that the ego will get an idea of how to shape your personality to keep you alive based on the two available programs it has. It will stay in the observation mode for the first seven years of your life since those years are influenced by your soul. For the first seven years, your soul and your ego share your heart chakra until the ego descends into your third chakra, making itself a comfortable nest and emerging as your personality. This is the beginning of the Fibonacci sequence (1, 1).

The ego only has two programs available to choose from; it is either a victim or a bully. Each has specific functions you need to fully understand since knowledge is power. If you leave your judgment aside and dive in, you quickly identify what your program is. The good news is that you could consciously change it and use your ego for your benefit. Your ego will stay with you for the rest of your physical life because it is an equal part of you. The ego will just mature into an intelligent mind. Imagine that it functions as your sweet little pet that you love unconditionally. He/she will play according to your rules and do anything to make you happy.

CONSCIOUS ACTIONS

The first step is becoming conscious of your ego's feelings and actions and identifying them without hurting emotions (now I am acting like a victim, now I am acting like a bully).

You want to watch your ego like a hawk, as the ego is a master trickster. The victim and bully programs can easily fluctuate back and forth, choosing to be one or the other to help you in particular life situations.

Understand that the ego has a tough job to do. It is a lone wolf, wild, wounded, and dangerous, protecting his territory by all means, but you can win his trust and tame him. You can tame your wild animal within, whether you call it a wolf, chameleon, turtle, or anything else.

Once you become fully aware of your ego, you have reached Fibonacci sequence number 2 (remember that you can quickly move back and forth in the Fibonacci sequence until you stabilize yourself). You could get stuck in the circle of up-and-down experiences (soul—ego).

After the awakening, the ego will let you grow spiritually to some degree; however, it will still want to stay in control. If you still feel like you need to be in control or have spiritual ups and downs, it is time to tame your ego, which means being conscious of your actions and learning to be in neutral energy.

THE EGO CHOOSES A PROGRAM

The story below exemplifies how the ego will choose the right program for you. There are many stories, and you have your very own. You could write down your life story and what happened to you so you can reflect on it and heal. We hear you, feel your pain, and send you unconditional love.

Two children from two different birth families who lived in other parts of the world experienced the same kind of childhood for the first seven years of their lives. The father was an alcoholic and constantly yelled at his wife. He hit her on occasion as well. He yelled at his children often and always found something wrong with them. He gave physical punishments or emotionally tortured them. The mother was sad and showed a victim pattern. She felt that she could not leave her husband. She gave him reasons and excuses, promising he would get better.

Each of these children (living in different birth families, in other countries) were secretly angry, but they could not express it well. They wished their father would change, wished their mother would find the courage to leave him. They both feel guilty because they thought it must have been something they did that caused their fathers to act like that. They blamed themselves.

One child started to hide more, became quieter, and tried to withdraw from the world. If he could, he would become invisible. When someone, like a teacher at school, noticed this child, he started to feel uncomfortable, maybe blush, or develop anxiety or low self-esteem, making him a prime target for bullies. Most of the time, he held all the anger, shame, guilt, and humiliation quietly inside of him, but these emotions secretly tortured this child every day. This child was brilliant and excelled at school, yet others quickly got ahead of him. He started to believe that something was wrong with him, that he did not deserve a good life or love. His human ego had chosen the victim program. Eventually, he would blame everyone for his failures. He will self-sabotage his own happiness. Sadly, a life of suffering will bring certain levels of comfort to this child because suffering will work as self-punishment.

The other child became more aggressive and started to rebel. Based on memories from past lives, some refuse to bow down to a bully and become bullies themselves. It is an animal survival instinct of the ego. In this child's mind, no one will hurt him, physically or emotionally, because he will do something first before anyone even tries. Bullies are victims first; however, the victim mentality is too much for their nervous system to take because they have lots of anger. The anger "upgrades" the program to bully, making the body survive and function in society. This child is determined that no one will ever make him feel like his father is making him feel. He will slowly grow an invisible "thick-shelled" barrier and not let many emotions inside. His human ego has chosen the bully program so this child will be louder and dominant. He will want to be the best in everything and will not care if he has to cheat to achieve his goal. He will act like he knows everything and will torture everyone around him. He will think he is happy because he gets what he wants and will constantly be in control.

Both boys grew up to be rather difficult individuals to deal with. One blames everyone else for his problems, and the other always believes he is right; both make the people around them miserable. It is important to remember that once upon a time, they were tiny little babies filled with divine unconditional love who had no control over what program the ego would choose. Since then, they have just learned to cope with it to survive.

VICTIM PROGRAM

Physical energy: The victim could be described as an underdog, often taken advantage of. He is a hard worker, giver, master survivalist, and chameleon who can adjust to fit his surroundings and be invisible.

The victim always needs to hype up his physical energy and requires a lot of inspiration to achieve something. This is very physically and emotionally exhausting daily.

The victim is an industrious individual who can convince himself to achieve something, and just when it is happening, everything falls apart. He has to start over. Often, you will hear him say, "I try so hard, and when I finally reach what I want, something bad happens, and I have to start all over again." Or, "I am afraid to feel happy because something bad is going happen." or, "Everyone thrives around me, except me. I am like a good luck charm to everyone except myself. I am so tired of this." Some people see victims as lazy, but in reality, victims are just paralyzed by the fear of failure and are tired of trying.

Emotional energy: Victims operate primarily from the right side of the brain, creative, feminine energy. The victim is a fantastic dreamer who hardly achieves his dreams for fear of possible humiliation. He battles with fears of failure and fears of success. He procrastinates, makes excuses often, self-sabotages himself, and is stuck in a poverty state of mind (even if he is rich). The victim secretly dreams that someone will save him. He cannot see his dreams come true because he subconsciously believes he is unworthy of being abundant, loved, successful, and happy. He has poor self-discipline, drowning in feelings of fear, guilt, shame, humiliation, and despair. He has low self-confidence and low self-esteem. Victims turn into unconscious psychic vampires when constantly complaining. Victims usually lack self-love and will doubt themselves all the time. He is consumed by quiet hate, anger, and jealousy, even though many victims will argue to the end that this is not true.

Many famous and successful people are secretly consumed by the victim program. For example, fear of failure, judgment, stage fright, fear that someone will discover who they are behind closed doors and that they are not as perfect as the world may think. They experience real fear of humiliation. Sadly, sometimes people commit suicide to escape their victim's ego. Suicide is not a permanent solution but rather another soul wound that will need healing in the next lifetime.

All this is nonsense; you can be who you want to be. If who you are comes from your heart, you would not need to impress anyone or be perfect. Unfortunately, way too many people find a temporary peaceful state of mind in drugs, prescription medicine, and alcohol, which helps them forget for a little while. Who leads you to these substances? Your ego does, so it can easily control you. Do we have your full attention?

Eva's note: To understand the next step, I want to share that the Pleiadians had worked with me for about a year before writing this chapter, giving me notes and exercises to consciously grasp the victim/bully program. They also guided me toward suitable sources of knowledge. My friend and true teacher Ann taught me how to recognize these programs and heal life patterns. I was guided to read the book The Eye of the I, From Which Nothing is Hidden, by David R. Hawkins and to study the Map of Consciousness that David Hawkins shared in his book. I practice this on my clients and on myself with great success. Now, the Pleiadians and I can share this with you.

THE PATTERN OF A VICTIM – NEW JOB

This is just an example, as there are many other scenarios. These steps will help you see how the program of the victim operates and how it can be changed.

1. You are stuck at a job you do not like. You need to make more money and would like to work in a better environment where you feel appreciated and supported.
2. One day, after a total meltdown, you finally get **angry** at yourself and at your current job and find the **courage** to say to yourself that you will apply for a new job. You feel **joy**! You are **overexcited**! You start making plans, **dreaming** of your new job and how awesome it will be. You are so encouraged and flooded with positive thoughts. If you have an imaginative mind, you totally picture what is happening as if it were a fairy tale coming true.
3. At your current job, you become more miserable than ever. You have the perfect fairy tale about your new job, but this job is holding you back before you can even apply for the new position. You will awaken energy or a sense of **pride** about how you are too good for your current workplace, becoming **boastful** (even if it's just in your mind) of how your work performance is perfect. You may even become **arrogant** toward your boss.

4. You start making reasonable **excuses** as to why you cannot apply for this new job. They need you at your current job because you are doing something no one else can do. Your commute will be longer, and you will have to wear a work uniform, which may be uncomfortable.

5. Someone at your current work will make you feel good about yourself, and you start to think, "Is it really worth it? Shouldn't I just stay?" Your ego happily supplies "yes" for you. **You let go of your dreams and settle for what you have.** You feel calm and peaceful for a while; this is where you belong. At this point, you can blame someone else and supply a few good victim comments such as, "Because my parents were poor, they could not give me a better education, "or "Because my husband is not supportive," etc.

6. You remain calm, will try to do your work the best you can, assist others, and do extra work without pay. Then, it all emotionally piles up again, and you become angry. The whole pattern then **repeats** itself.

Now, look at a few keywords from the pattern above and notice how one progresses to the other. Do not just read these words; feel them in your whole body, especially your heart and lower abdomen.

Anger – courage – joy - overexcited - dreaming – pride – boastful – arrogant – excuses – let go of your dreams and settle for what you have – repeats.

Now, compare the energy of the words with those below. What feels better to you?

Anger – courage – emotionally neutral – willing – safe - unconditional love – grateful - research – gain knowledge – address all the fears – it is worth it and so are you – positive - apply for a job – feeling neutral – trust - received new job – changed your victim pattern.

THE HEALING PATTERN OF A VICTIM

1. You are stuck at a job you do not like. You need to make more money and would like to work in a better environment where you feel appreciated and supported.

2. One day, after a total meltdown, you finally get **angry** at yourself at your current job and find the **courage** to apply for a new job. You will stay **emotionally neutral** about this because when you get overexcited, you tend to burn all your creative energy and then get tired. You are **willing** to put all your effort into this. You start making plans and a list of what you would like your new job to be like. You are flooded with positive thoughts and discourage yourself from thinking about your past

failures or how excellent this job will be. You know what you want, and you know it will be great.

3. At your current job, you become more miserable than ever. You clearly see that this is not working for you anymore and need to keep reminding yourself that it is **safe** to change your work. Your human ego is terrified. You send **unconditional love** to everyone and anything at this job every day. You are **grateful** for the opportunity you had. This work is just a bridge to something better and will end soon. There is someone else who is waiting for this job and will love this job as much as you will love your new one.

4. You are aware of your fear of failure and your fear of success, and you will not let any low-vibration feelings that are based on the past bring you down. You stay neutral while doing your **research** about the new job. If you need to enroll in school to **gain the knowledge** you need for the job, you will plan for it accordingly, and you will do it. You will acknowledge all the "excuses" for not getting that new job and **address all the fears** behind them. This part can take a few days or even a few years, but if a new job is what you want, **it is all worth it, and so are you**!

5. You are learning to stay **positive** because you have changed how you relate to your current coworkers' negative comments. It does not upset you anymore. You know that you are moving forward from this work and the old pattern of the victim. You are ready to **apply for a new job**. You know you are qualified, and you feel a healthy self-esteem about your energy and the work you have put toward making this decision. You will still stay **feeling neutral**. It does not matter if this company hires you; otherwise, the Universe could have another company in mind for you. The Universe may be testing you (this is normal) to see if you graduated from the victim pattern. **Trust**!

6. You have been **hired for a new job**! Now, it is time to celebrate. Be joyful, complete, and ecstatic! Acknowledge all you have done for this transformation! You have **changed your victim pattern**.

After all this joy you will feel, watch that you stay neutral instead of falling into the energy of pride and the program of a bully who "knows it all." Feel secure and good about yourself. Perform your work with honesty and integrity that benefits everyone. Refrain from comparing yourself to others and strive to live from your heart.

In conclusion, the victim program becomes terribly overwhelmed by change, causing anxiety, depression, and panic attacks. Fear of failure and fear of success make this program effective. Your ego will let you use affirmations and meditations. It will give you courage and allow you to get excited and happy about the changes you would like to make in your life. It will assist you in being a "forever dreamer," but it will lead you into overdrive of your emotions (like an engine overheating). After you exhaust your emotional energy, you will have an emotional crash into low feelings of guilt, hopelessness, humiliation, and shame. Then, as your best friend, it will give you a helping hand to pick you up again.

A way out of the victim program is to neutralize your emotions regarding the past and the future. Then, you can face your fears and activate your willingness to become a doer instead of a dreamer. Learn to love yourself. Define what safety and feeling safe mean to you. Trust yourself and consciously transform your inner anger into creative fire energy.

BULLY PROGRAM

Physical energy: The bully can be described as an overachiever, often with good self-discipline. He seems to be high in energy, and his success inspires others. But this energy is tricky and self-serving because it feeds his already inflamed ego with pride. He is a good speaker who can twist your words against you, convincing you he is right. He is a poor team player. Monetary wealth is significant because it makes the bully feel safe. He can earn a lot of money and lose a lot of money, having financial highs and lows throughout his life.

The people involved in the bullying program feel entitled to a good life for various reasons. These could be hard work, good luck, inheritance, or being born into a privileged family. However, it's important to note that being born into a privileged family does not automatically lead to becoming a bully; many individuals from such backgrounds become victims themselves.

The bully may also face financial struggles but often boasts about future success, such as owning a mansion next week. They are driven by success and may present themselves as team players, but their well-being is their top priority. Their attitude is often "My way or the highway." They tend to be loud and intimidating, seeking to control every situation. Bullies meticulously plan and execute their actions, whether it's a business deal or accusing their partner of cheating. In the bully's mind, they are always "right."

Emotional energy: The bully operates primarily from the left side of the brain, as well as logic and masculine energy. The bully is a psychic vampire. Sadly, many bullies are consciously aware of this ability and use it for their benefit. The bully has obsessive behaviors and must always be in control. Sometimes, the bully has no shame or needs to follow ethical rules.

In early childhood, the bully activated a robust self-protection mechanism. He grew an invisible shell, like a turtle. This shell serves to hide his low self-esteem, fear, and worries and creates emotional safety, a comfortable place where one can hide his true feelings. No one will ever see them or reach them and use them against him. He intimidates others, and if someone gets too close to see his weaknesses, he redirects the attention to somewhere other than himself.

The bully lives in denial and has trust issues. He is afraid of being a victim, poor, or dependent on others. He has a difficult time asking for help from his heart. It is easier for him to boss people around to do his bidding. He is obsessed with his social status and what people think of him.

The bully is afraid of deep emotions, opening himself up to anyone, or giving unconditional love. This is because the little kid within him never wants to hurt again. His definition of self-love is, "Me, myself and I." in a very unhealthy way. He prefers controlling/needy relationships where he can be in control so he will not get emotionally hurt. The bully is often angry, stubborn, short-fused, and not afraid to speak his mind. He blames everyone quickly, has secret regrets, and has a lot of cravings. Nothing is ever enough. The bully is unwilling to compromise because he battles secretly with the fear of failure.

THE PATTERN OF BULLY – OWNING A BUSINESS

This is just an example; there are many other scenarios. These steps will help you see how the bully's program operates and how it can be changed.

1. You are a skilled, hardworking carpenter, and you feel that your current **boss does not appreciate** all **you** know or all you do. You are irritated by listening to his nonsense. He makes you angry, and you refuse to agree with his point of view. You want to start your own business.

2. You quit your job and **accept responsibility** for creating your business.

3. Family members are **trying to help you** with ideas on where to advertise, possible clients, and how to set up your business. You appreciate their help, but in your mind, **they know nothing** about carpentry or how this should be done, so you decline their help. You are more stressed, yelling and making everyone feel **uncomfortable** around you.

4. You go into your turtle shell and brainstorm everything **alone** because you know everything about this new business idea. You **trust only yourself**. You leave your family and friends out. You work extra hours, getting little sleep. You are tired and frustrated but **driven by pride** that you can do this. Family members are just quiet around you. They stop asking you questions or offering to help. They get out of your way so you can do what you were "born" to do.

5. You launch your new business and book your first three projects. You will work up to twelve hours daily and refuse to hire someone to help you. You are watching your budget, but you are more afraid that the help will not do a good job. You have **no time or energy**

left for your family. You feel they do not understand how hard you work and how you do everything for them. You may be **feeling unappreciated**, but you **got what you wanted**.

6. You try to do your best, but eventually, your exhaustion and unhappiness catch up with you again. You will feel unappreciated, irritated, and angry, and your business may struggle. You will **repeat** the pattern all over again with different ideas or different angles on your business.

Now, look at a few keywords from the pattern above and notice how one progresses to the other. Do not just read these words; feel them in your whole body, especially your heart and lower abdomen.

The boss does not appreciate you—angry—you want—accept responsibility—family trying to help you—they know nothing—stressed—uncomfortable—alone—trust only yourself—tired—driven by pride—new business—no time or energy—feeling unappreciated—got what you wanted—repeat.

Now, compare the energy of the words with those below. What feels better to you?

The boss does not appreciate you – angry – you want – neutralize – observe – figure out – planning –

knowledge – accept responsibility – neutral energy instead of judgment – appreciation –gratitude - learning to guide others instead of bossing them – trust – new ideas – rejuvenates – willing – synchronicity – you are guided- service to humanity – honest – trustworthy – fair – people love you – your business if thriving- changed your bully pattern.

THE HEALING PATTERN OF BULLY – OWNING A BUSINESS

1. You are a skilled, hardworking carpenter, and you feel that your current **boss does not appreciate** all **you** know or all you do. You are irritated by listening to his nonsense. He makes you **angry**, and you refuse to agree with his point of view. **You want** to start your own business.

2. You **neutralize** all your emotions regarding work. You will **observe** your anger to **figure out** what you secretly fear and what you feel you cannot control. Then you start **planning** before you give a notice of leave at your job. You are set firm about your own future business. If you need to gain any **knowledge** regarding the operation of your new business, you will learn or seek the assistance of someone skilled in the profession. You **accept the responsibility** of creating your own

102

business. You talk to your family about how this may change family life, your calling to have your own business, and your desire to spend quality time with them.

3. Since family members are trying to help you, you will hold yourself in **neutral energy instead of judgment**. You accept their assistance and give them each responsibility to help according to what you think they can do. You express your **appreciation** and **gratitude** for everyone helping you. You hold your need to tell everyone how to do things. You are **learning to guide others instead of bossing them** and micro-managing them. You are learning to **trust**. You are open to **new ideas**, friends, and connections. Even though you work long hours and are tired, you prioritize family time. This **rejuvenates** you.

4. Instead of going into your metaphorical turtle shell, you are **willing** to listen to other people's ideas and implement them with yours. You notice **synchronicities** and acknowledge them. You realize **you are guided** on your path to start a new business and trust to follow this path. You give your notice at work because you know you can do this. After all, you want to help people live in nice houses (to be in **service to humanity**), and you know how hard it is to find **honest, trustworthy**, and **fair** contractors. You have all these qualities.

5. You launch your **new business**, book your first three projects, and need help. You hire temporary help,

someone your friend recommended. Your new helper has the same work ethic as you do. You acknowledge it and express your gratitude. You are no longer doing the work the way you think is best without considering what your consumers asked for. You gently guide them toward making the right choice regarding their projects. 6. You stay in the calm stage. **People love you**. They recommend you to their friends. **Your business is thriving**, your family and you feel happy. You are ready to hire more people, extending your business. You **changed your bully pattern**.

You know how to be successful; now it is time to do it right. Embrace your wholeness, and become a conscious, living frequency holder of any higher vibration energy you feel strongly connected to. Make your workplace or home a temple of light and watch that you stay humble. Treat people how you wish to be treated, and you will be living your mission to make this world a better place.

In conclusion, the bully program thrives on feelings of pride and unhealthy self-love. However, these energies also activate your destructive power. You spend long periods being upset, working hard to keep the materialistic lifestyle you define as part of your happiness. When you become sick or poor, there is no one to give you a helping hand because you have been pushing people away throughout your whole life. You are stubborn and not willing to compromise. This is often manifested as an illness, divorce, or a tragic event, which could serve as an awakening trigger.

The way out of the bully program is to neutralize your emotions regarding the past and the future. Then you start facing your hidden fears, taking off your protective shell, and learning to trust people and energy. Learn to love yourself for who you are. Define what safety and feeling safe means to you and work consciously on transforming your inner anger into creative fire energy.

CHAPTER 6

TOOLS
FOR THE EGO TRANSFORMATION

First, remember that your ego is your best friend, loving pet, and helper. You are teaching your ego new tricks and teaching it to feel safe. Feeling safe is the most essential energy the victim and the bully programs must master to overcome different fears. This is the main reason why we (the Pleiadians) acknowledge the ego before much else. We will spend quite some time reviewing it before we go into the story of your soul wounds. Even though we know you would prefer your soul's story first, this topic must be covered before we can proceed.

The transformation of your ego does not involve banishing it forever, much less getting rid of it completely. Rather, it involves learning to work with your ego. You will have to willingly accept it as your helper. It is equal to one-third of you. Ego + Soul = You

The ego fears letting you rise into your throat chakra, which is Fibonacci sequence number 3. This is because it believes it will die if it allows this to happen, as it genuinely believes that your body will die with it.

The ego knows you will start relating to situations differently, becoming reasonably positive. You will overcome your fears, although according to the ego's program, you can die by doing this (however, this is untrue). Fear is good for the ego because fear has kept humankind alive for thousands of years. The transformation process is a relatively safe, proven program. Can you see the ego's struggle? It is a tiny little ant projecting a big shadow on the wall, afraid you might figure out its trickery. Understand that your ego is trying to trick you out of this transformation.

The ego governs your first three chakras. The Base and Solar Plexus chakras dominate the physical (ego) energy. The Sacral chakra is dominant in the cosmic (soul) energy, but the ego's energy controls it. The first chakra (the need for survival) and third chakra (your mature self) squash your second chakra, which blocks creativity. It will be significantly controlled if not blocked since the ego's energy is trying to protect your survival.

So take a deep breath and assure your ego that you are not going to die and that you are both safe. Let it know that you are not shutting it out. You are going to learn to work with your ego on equal terms. You need your human ego to write a book, cook, or do gardening. You want the ego to allow your soul to consciously guide you, allowing your creative energy to be activated. You can make your "three-wheeled car" (your soul, ego, and you) move forward.

Building a Safe Nest for your Ego

Survival is the first chakra's work. Find a place that you enjoy and feel safe in. It may be your backyard, a specific room in your house, a closet, or any other place you like. Do not imagine a place; it must be physical.

This place will become your safe nest, even if only for a minute or two a day. Once again, you need to find a physical place because you will work with your first chakra, powered by physical (ego) energy. You need to message your physical body that you are safe.

Calm your mind. With your eyes open, you will physically keep yourself in the present. Think, "I am safe." Take several deep, slow breaths and consciously think, "I am safe. I can take care of myself. I can protect myself." Etc. You can chant out loud the phrase:

"I am safe."
In the musical notes
"E" – "C" – "D"
I (E)—am (C)—safe (D)

Do not let your ego or your thoughts talk to you now. During this exercise, you are entirely safe and have no problems. No issues, no bills to pay, nothing else to do. During this moment, you are altogether safe. Feel it, feel it, and feel it in your present body. Do not just think it; feel it. How does it feel to be safe and have no issues or problems? This statement is one hundred percent accurate at the moment, for the few seconds or minutes you sit there. Breathe this feeling into your body and first chakra and teach your body how it feels to be completely safe.

At first, you may be able to do this exercise only for a few seconds. Over time, you can work for up to a few minutes. It is a challenge, but it is rewarding and healing to teach your body how to feel safe without a need to be in control. Repeat this exercise a few times a week until it is easy to hold the "I am safe" frequency within your body. When it becomes second nature, a new program has been set.

While you get accustomed to feeling safe, look at your life. What makes you feel secure, and what does not. Do you need to disconnect from things, people, or behaviors threatening your life? Do you need to create a new, safe environment? Ask your ego and soul to assist you in this life transformation. Take it day by day. Completely trust yourself and the divine. You are always guided and loved. Feeling safe will allow your nervous system to relax and have more neutral energy.

NEUTRAL ENERGY

The second chakra's job revolves around emotional energy. It reflects in your fourth and sixth chakras, which are all cosmic (soul) energy chakras.

Neutral energy is the first higher vibration energy you should consciously reach. People with victim or bully programs often miss this step when reaching a higher energy. Because they have missed this neutral step, they will eventually fall from higher energies such as willingness, acceptance, love, joy, and peace when something goes wrong.

Neutral energy is a level of safety where one does not need to worry about momentary emotions, events from the past, or what will happen in the future. Neutral energy is a moment in the present time. It is a powerful stabilizer in the ocean of terrorizing emotions. Staying neutral is like walking through a minefield you created without harm. You know the correct path, and you know you are safe. You must fully trust your inner GPS. Bombs are exploding left and right, but you know you will be fine if you follow the set path. You are not scared or excited; you just walk from point A to point B. Whenever you are in an emotionally difficult life situation, stabilize yourself with neutral energy, and you will know your next step without your ego influencing you.

STAYING NEUTRAL - TOOL

You can try this mental exercise if you cannot quiet your mind and stay neutral. Focus on one object, for example, a pen. Stare at the pen for at least one minute; focus all your thoughts on this pen and not other things, such as what happened this morning or what you are doing tonight. It is only a pen; you look at it and nothing else. After you are done, consciously acknowledge that you can hold your focus and think nothing other than the pen. You can soon repeat this in longer sequences, without a tangible object, just with your mind.

You can go outside and hold your thoughts on a tree, repeat the same exercise, or gaze at the ocean. You can also try this by chanting an "Om" sound, focusing only on the sound with a little quiet time between breaths. You should be able to do this for about 10 minutes daily, with great focus. Soon, you will realize that you can quickly quiet your mind.

QUICK RELEASE FROM FEAR AND ANXIETY - TOOL

Your third chakra's job is to guide you through life, providing you with the confidence you need. When you have a hard time making a decision or experience fear or anxiety, put your left hand on the back of your head and hold it there. Position your right hand, pointer finger, and thumb above the center of each eyebrow and massage gently. Imagine your energy connecting from the back of your head to your frontal lobe. Think about the specific fear/or anxiety you just experienced; think about it as vividly as you can while gently massaging the points at the top of your eyebrows. This will bring blood to the frontal lobe of the brain. Once your brain has oxygen, you will start feeling calmer. It will also give you a sense of clarity over your situation.

QUICK RELEASE FROM FEELINGS OF SHAME, GUILT, AND HUMILIATION - TOOL

When you experience torturous feelings such as shame, guilt, or humiliation, gently press the tip of your nose and hold it for about two minutes or until the feelings go away.

The tip of your nose is a connection point between the central and governing meridians, which control the nervous system in your physical body. The central and governing meridians feed into each other in a circular motion. The central meridian is more sensitive to your emotional energy (becomes super sensitive when you awaken). The governing meridian is more sensitive to your physical energy. The tip of your nose is a doorway into these two meridian pathways that govern the nervous system. As you already know, emotions significantly affect the nervous system. The nervous system sends appropriate signals to the organs, eventually manifesting blockages, illnesses, etc.

While gently pressing the tip of your nose, you separate the energy line so that these two meridians cannot clearly communicate. They will stop circulating feelings, for example, if you feel ashamed. Think about it: When you feel ashamed, you feel it in your whole body. Your nervous system spreads this information through your body using these two meridians' pathways.

Anger

Anger is like fire. It just needs to be understood. Losing control of something important to you may elicit feelings such as anger, frustration, and anxiety. Needing to control something or everything is a form of hidden fear. As you already know, fear is one of the original programs in the human body which ensures survival. Therefore, control rises from fear. It works simply. Instead of fearing something, you learn to control it. For example, you become angry when you are threatened because you are losing your job, social position, status, house, health, or someone you love. Your human ego convinces you that you are right to want to be in control and get what you want. In a way, your anger is justified. For the ego, it is easier to keep you angry rather than to accept the fear of failure, which leads to deep feelings of shame and guilt, which can lead to possible suicide. This is a state the ego likes to keep you in because you are easily controllable. Your ego will do anything to protect you so that you do not die prematurely until your assigned journey in this lifetime is completed.

THE ANATOMY OF ANGER

When your anger escalates beyond your control, your body is designed to protect your survival. It will release adrenaline, creating an energy rush. This is called your "fight or flight" response. It can be good or bad for you because you are not thinking with your logical brain now. Your spiritual brain is in total darkness, and you are acting based simply on your survival program, hyped up on adrenaline.

Anger may save your life in life-threatening situations but will do nothing for your spiritual growth.

In the physical body, anger dominates in your first three chakras. Anger energy thrives on negative emotions such as lust, greed, jealousy, desire, pride, shame, guilt, insecurity, and low self-esteem.

Chakras affected by anger:
First charka – survival – physical (ego) energy
Second chakra – childhood emotions, creativity, sexuality – cosmic/spiritual (soul) energy

Third chakra – self-awareness, grown-up self – physical (ego) energy

Two chakras use physical (ego) energy, while one uses cosmic (soul) energy. The second chakra is your creativity. Under stress, your body creates adrenaline to give you a physical tool to physically dodge what may look like a threat to your body (either threatening your survival or your grown-up self). It does not discriminate between someone threatening you emotionally or physically. Your body is brilliant and yet incredibly dumb at the same time. It does not recognize any difference. It responds to your original, emotional thoughts (2nd, 4th, 6th chakras) and acts accordingly to protect you. Your natural creativity, a creative fire in your second chakra, may be squashed by these physical (ego) chakras. Yet, you need all three to work together to create the catalyst for transformation.

This transformation could be compared to the old legend of the Phoenix from ancient Egypt. You must create a safe, ingenious, and abundant nest for your physical being and then metaphorically set it on fire, detaching emotionally from your materialistic possessions to give birth to your creative self.

Imagine if you could consciously control this incredible amount of energy. We will call it your fire energy. Fire could be your worst enemy since it can create extensive damage, activating your destructive power, or it could be your best friend and activate your creative power. It can be gentle, warm, and helpful. It can be your baby firebird.

Taming the Fire - Tool

The activation stellar cycle of 2012 opened you spiritually to the work relating to and with conscious energy. Conscious work is used instead of hypnosis and is the most profound energy work of your time.

When you feel angry, try to consciously acknowledge the situation, "I am angry because I cannot control this or that (name your specific situation here)."

This is a critical point in your healing process. Next, you have to become an active doer, which means that you will process this mentally by shifting your perspective and physically through your body by doing something. Sometimes, it is hard to calm down and go about your day. Your body may be high in adrenaline, and you may need to physically release it to feel better and process it mentally.

Consciously acknowledge that you cannot control everything. Pick one or all of the physical tools we suggest below.

If you feel like you are going to explode with overwhelming anger, which can make you say or do something that you will later regret, do something physical like:

- Clean the house.

- Cut the grass.
- Go for a run.
- Go to a gym.
- Take a walk.
- Lock yourself in the bedroom (no need for an audience), and hit the pillow as much as you need to.
- Go to a place where no one can hear you and swear as much as you like.
- If you live in a deserted place, scream at the top of your lungs and let it all out.

Whatever you choose, turn your anger into a physical task instead of unleashing your anger and frustration on anyone. Exhaust yourself until you feel your anger subside. Surrender. Surrendering does not mean giving up; it is a path to your power without a fight.

FINDING THE ROOT OF YOUR ANGER - TOOL

The next time you start feeling anxious or angry (before you get livid), take a mental step back and look at the situation without any judgment or emotional involvement (I want this outcome to be my desired way) and start asking yourself questions like:
- "Why am I angry?"
- "What is it that I cannot control right now?"
- "What is it that I am afraid of?"

Create a journal and write down your responses. Do not overthink things; just write the first thing that comes to mind. There is nothing silly about this. This inner conversation with yourself about why you are angry is only to help you understand the root of this problem. When you consciously understand, you can shift your perspective on the situation. You can change the way you think about it or how you perceive it. When you are ready, accept it all.

After you accept the issue, forgive yourself. Whatever you are angry about, forgive yourself, then forgive the person or people you are angry at. Forgive yourself for failing in some aspects. Do it in your heart; have a good cry over it. If you struggle with the question, "Can I forgive? Can I let it go?" Then ask yourself this: "How long will I torture myself over it?" "How long will I hold this anger inside of me?"

It is easier to forgive yourself and others than to be stuck here for another century while holding a grudge.

FAIRNESS

Once you settle down a little bit after an episode of being upset or anxious, go back to your journal. Again, write why you were upset. Now ask these different questions:
- How can I handle this situation differently?

- How can I shift my perspective about this?
- How did the other person (who triggered you) feel? What is going on in that person's life that I may or may not understand now?

AND
- Do I have to have the last word/action?
- What is fair?

"What is fair?" is the most important question of all.

Fairness is a neutral point and should become your internal GPS when you are upset or need to decide or solve a difficult situation.

fairness = neutral energy

Example: You're at your favorite store, and you find a pair of shoes on sale for 50% off. It is such a good deal, so you put a pair in your cart. You take a picture of the price tag on the shelf. At the register, they scan for the total price. You politely ask the cashier to check the price, and she scans it again, giving you an uncomfortable look as she tells you there is no sale. This is a trigger to a victim, as victims will hold the embarrassment that will fire up the anger inside. They will purchase the shoes for the total price and feel horrible inside. This also triggers a bully who likes to be loud and raise their voice, demanding to see the manager, controlling the situation, and thinking that they are right. It does not matter which category you fall under; you can handle this situation differently, with dignity and fairness.

Take a deep breath before you react, take a mental step back, and ask, "What is fair?"

Fair:

1. There was a sign showing a sale for 50% off.

2. I took a picture and showed it to the clerk. If not, I can walk back to take a picture.

3. Mistakes happen.

Your steps coincide with fairness:

1) I correct the mistake without any emotional input from me (being upset about it, wanting it, or being rude to the clerk), and I will be neutral.

2) I decide how much I really want these shoes. If the sale applies, I would like to buy these shoes; if not, I may not want to buy them because I do not need them. The sale was my trigger to get them in the first place.

3) I handle this situation without feeling bad, embarrassed, or angry. The line behind me is just a line. I am doing an excellent job so that someone else does not have to deal with this situation again. Also, I help the store correct errors if the item is mistakenly discounted. By handling this situation calmly, I am in service to others.

Solution:

Without emotional input, you show the picture to the clerk, asking them to recheck it. You can politely express to the clerk what a good job/he/she is doing and even apologize for holding the line up. Remember that you already have a decision (if you want or do not want these shoes without a sale). If the answer is, "I am sorry we have made a mistake." You can give a calm smile and say, "That is ok, I wish they were on sale, but I understand that mistakes happen. I do not want them."

This is fair. You will feel good inside, and the clerk will feel good as well because you have not attacked her (with your inner upset energy or outspoken harsh words) with your desire to have these shoes.

If you fall under the victim pattern, you will feel a sense of accomplishment for speaking up for yourself. If you fall under the bully pattern, you will feel good about yourself for not yelling at the clerk.

Finding what is fair means disconnecting from your first and third physical chakras. If you disconnect from wanting these shoes, your beautiful charisma and creativity can solve the solution as peacefully as possible, with the best outcome for both sides. Metaphorically, you created a safe nest (decided what was fair), and when you burned it (carried it out), the solution came out like a baby firebird, pleasing everyone.

This scenario can be applied with variations to any aspect of your life that may trigger lower feelings.

KINDLING THE CREATIVE FIRE - TOOL

To use your creative fire energy positively, you must become an active doer instead of a complainer and a procrastinator. Set a goal, write down a to-do list (to achieve this goal) that you will follow every day, and keep yourself accountable for finishing it. Keep moving forward. Becoming a doer will rekindle the good physical fire (ego) energy in your first and third chakras. That fire will ignite your second chakra's cosmic (soul) energy, transforming the fire into a creative energy full of inspiration and new ideas.

This will help you move forward in your spiritual and physical transformation. Follow these three simple steps to use your creative fire in anything you do. Create from your heart, not from fear.

1. Calm your fear by bringing feelings of safety to your survival instinct and your grown-up self.

2. Stay emotionally neutral toward all situations and decisions.

3. Follow your inner GPS and decide based on what is fair.

WHEN THE NEW PROGRAM FINALLY REGISTERS

The tools needed for the ego's transformation will be reinvented (if used regularly) as new and productive programs that replace their negative counterparts in the body.

When you know the theory and exercises for it (and you consciously apply them in your transformation), you will wake up one day and experience an "AHA" moment where you really will "get it." It will also feel so easy. What you have read/learned/practiced will finally register within your body. It's like realizing you know your multiplication tables without thinking about it. It is programmed deeply in your mind, and there is a memory in your body! That is when the new program finally registers with your human body. It feels great, like a gentle electric current is running through your body, and you know you "got it." You know you can do this.

When learning or gaining new knowledge, the energy comes and leaves in horizontal motions in the form of feeling. To truly create energy memories of new knowledge (registering the new program), you need to connect feeling to knowing; thus, the energy comes in vertical motions as thoughts. When the horizontal and vertical energies meet, preferably at your heart chakra, the bells will metaphorically start to ring, and you will have an "AHA" moment.

feeling+knowing = manifesting

Your soul came from the stars, but you embody a human body. You can help program that body. You are learning to connect your star (extraterrestrial) energy with human energy. Repetition of a new habit (program), staying positive, and owning up to the latest "program" are the keys to maintaining your current human vessel. It takes patience and time, but it can be done.

POORLAND, RICHLAND, AND GOODLAND

A PARABLE OF THREE DIVERSE LANDS

Once upon a time, there were three nations, Poorland, Richland, and Goodland. Where one land ended, the new one began.

Each country lived separately. Only a few people ventured out beyond the borders. Mysterious stories were told by those who went and came back. Both Poorland and Richland thrived on the preset rules with deep-rooted beliefs. The rules were in place to ensure their survival and should remain unchanged, even when challenged. Seasons came and went, babies were born, and people died; everyone learned to be content in the place where they lived. Everyone, even in Poorland, believed their land was the best place to live.

One day, a traveler from a faraway land wandered into Poorland. Everyone stopped what they were doing to stare at the stranger. He did not fit in; there was something strange about him. Would he understand their rules?

Being poor was good. You had to work super hard for anything you needed. Dreams of a better life are dangerous because dreams do not come true.

People walked the streets in tattered, dirty clothes yet seemed content. They were proud of who they were. "This is how God made us," they said. "We grow our food and eat little. We do not have big machines to help us like in Richland, and we do not want them anyway. We sing, dance, and speak in a simple language, and we like it. We do not need fancy books and education to make us better. We are hardworking people. The world would end without us. We are good people. To be rich is not right! We hate Richland and all the people in it! They do not work as hard as us! Everything comes easy to them! They can keep their laundry machines and fancy food."

Out of nowhere, one child shouted, "It is not fair that God gave it to them and not to us!" Immediately, the elders scorned her. "We may be simple, but we are proud of who we are! Join us, fellow traveler, stay and live with us."

The traveler thought to himself, there must be more in this world. He thanked the good, hard-working people in Poorland for welcoming him and said, "I had a dream." before he could finish speaking, people started to scream frantically, "Dreamer! Be aware of the dreamer!" In a split second, the hospitality of the Poorland people turned into hostility. A mother guided her little girl to take a burning stick and burn this stranger who dared to dream of something better. Startled, the traveler looked at the innocent little girl whose mother conditioned her to hate anyone who wanted something more from life. Sadly, he understood that fear protected their survival, but dreams threatened it. The traveler ran and ran until he reached the bridge leading into Richland.

As he entered Richland, the traveler saw that life in Richland was spectacular. People wore beautiful clothes, had luxurious houses, and ate abundant delicious food. The traveler thought this was a good life that one could have. Immediately, he was offered a great job with a handsome salary, but under one condition. He would never communicate with Poorland. Poorland was poison, a threat to the people of Richland. People in Richland worked hard and were prosperous. Ambitions were encouraged. The school offered the best education one could imagine.

And so, it appeared they had everything. Life was good in Richland. One day, the traveler noticed something strange. Abundance was overflowing here, but fear was running the land. There were fears of becoming poor. There were fears of people from Poorland. The fear of who could come at any time and steal their possessions, as they did on occasion. The fear of losing the life they cherish. Even the fear that someone may have more than they have.

The traveler thought, "This cannot be the end of my journey; there must be something more. Both provinces lived in extremes—one extremely poor and one profusely rich—yet both were saturated in constant fear and anger. Couldn't they reach out to each other for help? Couldn't they love each other?"

He politely declined the offer to stay in Richland. Like in Poorland, hospitality turned into hostility, so the traveler ran for his life.

Lost on the road, he learned that people from Richland do not travel because they are afraid of robbers and sudden misfortunes. Only a few, very few traveled, who allowed themselves to dream that there must be something more than just Poorland or Richland. The traveler thought, "Could there be a land where you could live without fear and control? Could you be abundant? Could you be happy? Would you find the meaning to life?" As he dreamed his dream, he saw a light flickering far in the distance. It was a bridge with an illuminated sign that read "Welcome to Goodland."

As he crossed the bridge, he wondered what kind of land this was, only to see another sign, "Let go and let God." He saw a beautiful landscape with intelligent, eco-efficient houses. He saw happy people chatting, enjoying picnics in the meadow, and joyful kids running and screaming.

The traveler asked curiously, "Why is everyone so peaceful here? Why is there no one watching the bridge? Why is no one afraid of invaders from Poorland or Richland?"

"Everyone is welcome here," answered a beautiful woman beside him, "But not everyone likes to stay." She smiled at his confused expression. "We have successful businesses and advanced health care and can buy anything we want. We can travel the world. We have all we need. Yet that does not define us. We learned that anyone can be abundant, yet there is a difference. Our abundance streams from love; thus, it is everlasting. Love is the source that created this land, you see.

In Goodland, we are employed by God. Every morning, we quiet our minds and ask, how can I be of service to humanity? Each of us receives an assignment intuitively. We all get rewarded.

We put others ahead of ourselves. We are in service to humanity every single day. We live with joy and peace in our hearts. As with anywhere else, we have good and bad days, but we fully trust in God's consciousness that created us. We know that we do not have to be afraid of anything. When one thing ends, there is an opportunity for a new one to emerge. Those who come here with greed or need control do not thrive here. Sooner or later, they will leave, realizing this is not a happy land for them. This place offers profound realization and transformation to the soul-mind consciousness. Only when one is ready will one find their content place here. Each of us living here went through stages of poverty, richness, losing control, letting go, and finding God. We welcome everyone and hold no one. We know that some of our children, when they grow up, will desire to venture out into the other lands and learn their lessons. We also know that they may return one day. We encourage them to do so.

We extend our hospitality to you, traveler, to stay and live your dream. And if you desire to leave, we celebrate your decision and will set you out on your journey with enough food and money to last until you reach the next land."

That is how the traveler found Goodland, and he lived there happily ever after. And if he has not yet died, he is still happily living there.

~ The End ~

The moral of this story is that pride and fear are products of the ego and a need for control. Love transforms, heals, and nourishes dreams so that they may come true.

CHAPTER 7

THREE ORIGINAL SOUL WOUNDS

Your soul-mind consciousness is the author of your "Book of Life"—your guidebook for living on Earth. Its pages contain magnificent adventures, love stories, ancient knowledge, and learning lessons. They also include stories of unresolved physical and emotional pain, distress, and betrayals that caused your soul to suffer. You can call these your soul's wounds.

Three main periods created deep soul wounds:

-The destruction of Atlantis, choosing the Path of the Light or the Path of the Dark.

-The Essenes Community and the death of Jesus Christ.

-The Wise Women and Witch Trials.

Do you believe that past events that caused emotional pain may still affect you and create obstacles in your life today? They might be making you falsely believe that since you failed in the past, you are still a failure in your current life. Did you really fail? The truth is that everyone experiences failure. Perhaps failure was necessary for Earth's collective evolution and to help us to find our true selves.

Speaking on behalf of ancient ancestors, we failed not because we wanted to but because the circumstances were unfavorable to our success. In addition, we diverted from God's plan and occasionally employed our own. But did we fail completely? No. You have succeeded if you are still here, looking for answers on serving humanity and finding your way back home!

It helps to know that before the destruction of Atlantis, you had a choice to never come back. Yet you joined a great soul rescue mission and stayed here. Today, many of you feel finished and ready to return home. To make that happen, you need to heal all the wounds your soul has suffered on Earth since Atlantis.

There is a miraculous tool to heal these wounds. It's so simple that you'll laugh. It is a frequency of "unconditional love." Our Pleiadian brothers and sisters, Jesus Christ and Mary Magdalena, demonstrated the power of unconditional love while living on Earth.

DOOR INTO YOUR PAST – ENERGY EXERCISE

When learning about life after Atlantis and discovering your soul wounds, create an invisible door that vibrates with the frequency of unconditional love. That door will be your opening to those times. When you read these final chapters, always walk through this door to allow yourself the maximum soul healing.

1. Imagine this door is shaped like a diamond, leading to your past lives. Take a deep breath in and let it out. In your mind, you know that this door is made of the frequency of unconditional love.

Snap the fingers of your dominant hand on all sides of the door to clear the energy before stepping through its threshold. This will cleanse any lower energies.

Snap your fingers (above your head, below your belly, on your left, and then right) by saying:

As above,

So below,

As on the left,

So, on the right.

2. Imagine walking through its threshold, knowing and feeling that you have consciously stepped into the frequency of unconditional love!

3. Feel the frequency of unconditional love. Feel it in your whole body and go on your journey.

For those struggling to embrace unconditional love, think of something you love. It can be a place, pet, favorite food, thing, or person. Think of what you love and notice how it makes you feel in your body. Take this feeling and make it your threshold frequency.

Past Lives are Revealed in Dreams

Remembering your dreams and consciously healing your past lives will heal your soul wounds. This is the purpose of Fibonacci sequence number 5. Forgiveness, unconditional love, and divine light will illuminate your path ahead. This is the trinity for the healing catalyst you need.

Dreams are an essential part of your soul's communication with you. Your human aspect needs sleep to rejuvenate your physical body, but your soul does not.

In your dream state, your soul will take you on a journey to visit places you think do not exist. Past lives are shown to you in small fragments, pictures, or movie-like. Often, the most dramatic scenes are relived over and over. Your soul has no intention to torture you; it wants to show you what needs to be healed. Upon your awakening, you may think that you are having horrible nightmares. In a way, you are correct. You already lived that nightmare somewhere, and your soul still remembers it because it never forgets (if it left soul wounds). The soul wound manifests in your physical life as fear, which could physically show as anxiety, panic attacks, depression, hostility, apathy, and so on. In your dream state, your soul has a chance to remind you of what had happened to you, who you indeed are, or where you came from so you can become conscious to fully heal. Your ego does not want you to know this because it does not resonate with its survival program. Something that has left your soul wounded is a red flag for the ego. The ego is unaware that you do not have to repeat history or have the right to change it.

Some of you have dreams of your lives on distant planets. It's the actual home that you are dreaming about. Your soul is showing you this part of your origin so that you can regain memories and realize that you are not just an ordinary human being. You are a being of intelligence, benevolent light, and love, living in this primitive physical body, believing that this is your only life.

When you dream of Atlantis, you reach the core of your original, first soul wound on Earth. It may be painful, scary, or beautiful. It is your soul's imaginary door within, opening for you so you may walk in as a conscious embodiment of unconditional love and healing.

Your dreams and memories of Atlantis may vary depending on the path you have chosen after Atlantis, the Path of the Light or the Path of the Dark. There is no judgment; there is only healing and unconditional love.

Despite your path, you are all children of God and were all created equally with love and light.

There is a light within you that shines bright.
There is love within you, a love that created your life.
Life was created with love.
The light was given to protect this life.

*Love and Light are your original frequency,
and your birthright.*

CHAPTER 8

THE PATH OF LIGHT AND THE PATH OF DARK

PART 1 - THE PATH OF LIGHT

Master Thoth was walking through the ravaged ground of what used to be his beloved Atlantis. The fire was still alive and burning on the dry surface of the sand. The powerful blast that destroyed several islands of Atlantis had arrived, as Master Thoth had predicted in his vision. First, a massive geomagnetic storm hit Earth. The technology on Earth was temporarily disabled. Intergalactic communication was destroyed. Just a few days later, meteorites struck the Earth.

Before the powerful solar flares hit Earth, they caused the artificial intelligence (AI) located on the moon to malfunction. AI had served as a protective shield around Earth. Highly advanced AI technology has been utilized for thousands of years to change the course of any invading particles entering the Earth's moon's proximity. The AI was self-functioning and self-repairing, so no one believed malfunctions could occur.

When the meteorites reached the Earth's atmosphere, it caused great panic and shock to many.

The Sons of Belial were trying to revive all the lost technology quickly, but powerful explosions caused even more devastation.

Master Thoth remembered the day he first received inner guidance, which led him to explore the land in Egypt. He started preparing an escape from Atlantis 6,000 years before the final destruction. Initially, he thought his visions were not correct. How could someone or something destroy Atlantis? In his vision, he saw the sun shining brighter than he had ever seen, and then came a solar flare that collided with the Earth's atmospheric shield. It looked as though a light had bounced off of Earth's surface. It appeared to happen in slow motion, even though it actually only took a matter of seconds. The flare itself did not cause harm to any living organism, although it shut down all technology that existed in Atlantis at the time. It caused the sky to explode in an array of brilliant colors before an eerie silence enveloped Atlantis and its surrounding area.

After a period of silence, a powerful explosion would occur. He received inner guidance telling him that everyone should take refuge in the inner cities of Earth when this day comes and remain there until the storm is over. Children of the Law of One began to prepare for this day. The Sons of Belial only laughed. Master Thoth tried to tell everyone about his vision that all machines would malfunction one day, but only some believed in the possible failure of advanced AI technology.

During his life, Master Thoth had witnessed the overuse of technology, similar to what happened to the Lyrans before their planet was destroyed a hundred thousand years ago. He witnessed extraterrestrials living on Earth, abandoning the Universal Laws, and forgetting God. Those who fell under the spell of lower animal energies became ego-possessed. He knew that we could control many things, although nature and the Universe have their own minds. If you are in harmony with the Universe and nature, you walk with God. If you follow your ego, you must deal with the consequences. He shook his head; if you cannot change the essence of your being, the cycle will follow you. Suddenly, Earth felt so small and congested by greedy, ego-possessed extraterrestrials who suffered from the side effects of the animal DNA. They currently fought over territory, power, and the Earth.

His heart felt heavy over the loss of the civilization in which he (and others) had taught the language of love. He clutched the green, emerald tablet under his arm and signaled his group of devoted friends and students to start their travel toward Egypt.

The true Atlanteans (as Master Thoth lovingly called them), or the Children of the Law of One, followed the protocol of the Council of Light. The purpose of the Council of Light was to keep the Atlantean civilization a secluded project on Earth. Therefore, they did not interfere with other evolving organisms and had to relocate to Egypt. His mind had wandered to the splendid gardens of Atlantis, where he had spent hours meditating to connect with God's consciousness so that he could receive guidance on how to teach, co-create, and move forward. His physical heart was linked with that of his soul mate. Their bodily forms walked side by side. His emotions were overflowing with sadness, although he tried to bring unconditional love to the situation. This unconditional love gave him the strength to continue moving forward. This signified a new beginning that would undoubtedly test everyone.

THE BEGINNING OF THE PATH OF DARK

After the successful creation of the human/extraterrestrial body, the Sons of Belial proposed the creation of human slaves to take care of the heavy physical work that everyone did. The proposition was denied by the Council of Light, who monitored the Earth project.

Since the Earth was free to explore, various star groups began migrating to different parts of the relatively empty planet. The Sons of Belial were disappointed about the denial of their project. They did not take no for an answer and secretly worked on their project.

After the fall of Atlantis, seven central communities worldwide were led by extraterrestrials. Mesopotamia, Siberia, Egypt, South America, Australia (and New Zealand), India, and the Himalayas. The Sons of Belial favored the area of Mesopotamia.

EGYPT

The Children of the Law of One, or Master Thoth tribe, claimed Egypt as their first home after life in Atlantis.

It served as a mid-station (safe house) for many. Whether one stayed there for a few days, several years, or several lifetimes, it was a home and a secure base for the Children of the Law of One community.

When you awaken your starseed energy, many of you who walked on the Path of Light will remember fragments of ancient life in Egypt. You may feel deeply connected to ancient Egyptian teachings and search for information about the mystery schools. If you are experiencing some kind of emotion relating to this topic, you are most likely from the lineage of Master Thoth's tribe. Embrace the feeling and assist your human ego to feel safe.

Later, ascended masters (and many students who eventually became true teachers) often moved between Egypt, South America, and the Himalayas, as they were interconnected through inner passageways. They secretly assisted those who lived on the Path of Light in Mesopotamia. The movement between these communities led to the development of soul memories, which involved being in multiple places during the same period.

RIPPED DIMENSIONS

The explosion that caused the destruction of Atlantis was so powerful that it caused multiple dimensions to rip open. The second dimension suffered more damage than the others. Low-vibration entities that had never seen the surface of Earth (and previously had no access to physical bodies) were pouring into the Earth's dimension. They were flying around, much like maniacs high on drugs, possessing physical bodies to act out their desires. For these beings, having access to physical bodies had been the highest achievement of their lives. You had to have a physical body to create something physical, whether good or bad. Imagine someone who is not spiritual waking up in the morning and realizing they can create anything with their mind. That second-dimensional situation was much like that, but with more destruction. One day, these beings woke up and saw an open door that led them into the world of physical 3D. Of course, they were thrilled!

However, this was a living nightmare for the original extraterrestrials who had settled on Earth. Those who took the Path of Light could remove these beings from possessed bodies and return them to the second dimension. They successfully closed all the dimensions ripped open during the explosion, including the second. However, about 10% of the beings that entered from the second dimension could hide and remain on Earth undetected.

THE TEMPLE OF HATHOR

The Temple of Hathor was constructed to aid in spiritual and physical healing following the incident in the second dimension. All visitors to Egypt were required to visit the Temple for purification and revitalization, and it functioned much like a hospital.

The Hathors arrived on Earth at the beginning of the Atlantean period. They worked closely with fairies, elves, dragons, and other magical beings who were guided to live in the inner cities. The Hathors were masters of sound frequency healing. The sound they naturally produced (from their souls), when combined with crystal grids and healing energy, created an energy that caused second-dimensional beings to quickly leave the physical bodies that they possessed.

The chamber dedicated to this work was narrow with a high arched ceiling. There was a small device resembling a tall and narrow booth with two openings made of stone and crystal in the middle of the room. This device was used as a security checkpoint. One would step into the booth, which measured approximately one meter wide and four meters tall. Six Hathors, three at each opening of the device, would sing to your soul-mind consciousness and tune up your physical body to higher vibrations. Another three trained masters stood further away so that they would be able to isolate the second-dimensional entity when it was forced to leave the body.

Once the process started, every cell within your body would vibrate as if you were connected to electricity. For a short period, you would become paralyzed, although your body would be vibrating at a very high speed. You would entirely trust the Hathors. It felt safe to relinquish your control and surrender to the process. You would let them do the work because you knew they loved everyone unconditionally and would have the highest intentions for you. When the low-vibration entities detached from your body, trained masters would trap them and return them to their original dimension.

At the end of the process, one would collapse, weak and tired. When you were removed from the device, you were cleansed from negative entities. Walking forward through a door different from the one you entered, you were assisted by other Hathors and healers. They would lead you into the rejuvenation room in a different part of the Temple. There, you would spend as much time as needed until you felt strong again, as the cleansing process was often exhausting.

SLEEP PARALYSIS IN YOUR CURRENT LIFE

Following your own awakening, some of you may experience sleep paralysis. You may notice some extraterrestrial beings in your room or sense their energy. To you, this is a horrifying experience in which "you may think" that you might be under attack by dark alien beings.

We understand these situations may be scary or intimidating, as you do not know what may happen. Perhaps you feel as though you do not have any control, hence your possible inability to move or see what is around you. If this happens again, try to stay calm to determine if the extraterrestrials (who may be near you) are good or bad. Not everything is terrible. To prepare for this in advance, always keep a good rapport with your guides and soul family and learn to "test the energy" around you during frightening situations like these.

Notice that when you experience sleep paralysis or some temporary shocking experience in your physical body, your mind is conscious. Could you entertain the possibility that your soul family is trying to work with you now, wanting you to remain conscious so that you can remember their assistance? Soul healing is most effective when you are conscious. Healing the soul during deep sleep or through hypnosis is not very effective. Your soul family wants you to be aware of your energy and in charge of your own healing, whether it is soul healing or physical healing.

In many cases, sleep paralysis is a modern-day approach of your guides cleansing you from lower dimensional entities. It is very similar to the Temple of Hathor in Egypt. Remember, no one does anything against their free will in the spiritual world. You must have asked them for this cleansing before birth or in your soul contract. The experience may involve waking in the middle of the night, feeling paralyzed, and seeing or sensing the presence of other beings around you. Your body may vibrate; you may even feel levitating above your bed. Because you do not know what is happening, you may become afraid and experience terrorizing thoughts running through your mind. Those thoughts stem from lower energies that do not want to leave you (their excellent vessel). They want to keep you in a state of fear so that you might stop the removal process. Remember that you have free will, and these lower beings will try to manipulate you to keep themselves safe. If you experience this, do not freak out. Test the energy. Mentally ask these extraterrestrial beings if they are of the essence of unconditional love (if they have the highest intentions for you); ask three times as calmly as possible. If the answer is "yes" three times in a row, you can trust them and surrender to this experience. This will likely be the last time you experience sleep paralysis, as all the lower entities will be removed.

CONSCIOUS VS. UNCONSCIOUS ASSISTANCE

We want you to notice the difference between how your soul family works and how dark beings work with you. When you are experiencing sleeping paralysis, you are conscious, and eventually, by your free will, you become fully alert, and the paralysis stops. When or if you are experiencing an alien abduction, you are not conscious. You remember afterward. When you use alcohol or recreational drugs, you may have blackouts, and you are unconscious. These "blackouts" open the door to all negative beings that want to attach to you. You will realize that something does not feel right after you become conscious again.

Unseen energy is frightening because the ego constantly wants to be in control. Your soul family supports your open consciousness. Dark beings sneak in when you are unconscious, and your energy is open.

THE CREATION OF MYSTERY SCHOOLS

When the "Children of the Law of One" settled in Egypt, the Annunaki had already engineered many humans corresponding to their secret experiments and projects. The Anunnaki experiment, which originated during Atlantis (not after), got out of hand when they failed to keep their project contained and secret. All humans had limited memory of who they were, as their psyche was severely damaged from the genetic experiments. Therefore, when Master Thoth's tribe moved to Egypt (after the destruction of Atlantis), humans were already living among extraterrestrials.

Two major issues were classified as urgent. The first revolved around the temporary loss of our intergalactic transportation and communication. The second was what to do with all these human slaves.

The first problem started long before the destruction of Atlantis. Extraterrestrial wars occurred over a want for power. The planet Maldeck was destroyed due to nuclear weapons. Its destruction sent powerful shock waves throughout your Universe. Mars was affected the most, receiving quite a bit of destruction.

At the time, several dangerous experiments were taking place on Mars since it was the perfect place to hide experiments from the Council of Light. Mars served as an intergalactic transportation center for other distant planets. The shock wave from Maldeck disturbed Mars' electromagnetic field and its atmosphere. The artificial intelligence malfunctioned, and many weapons stored on Mars spontaneously exploded, destroying Mars' atmosphere. Many died instantly, and within a short time, Mars became uninhabitable.

The primary Intergalactic Transportation Center was destroyed. Life changed for us all, and we became temporarily stuck on Earth. Thankfully, our intergalactic communication was intact. We let our families know that we were okay on Earth. We asked them to build a new Intergalactic Transportation Center, although we knew it would be challenging since two planets had been destroyed. One was eradicated, the other covered in radiation and uninhabitable. We knew it would take a considerable amount of time until assistance arrived. We could not teleport (for example, from Earth to Pleiades) by the power of our own will.

When Atlantis was destroyed, our beloved home was destroyed, and our communication lines were disabled. We were truly stuck on Earth, not only with our anchored energy but also without intergalactic transportation and communication.

The second issue involved all the humans that the Annunaki had created. We were shocked to learn that (in a manner of speaking) they were our children who needed someone to teach them (we will explain in more detail later).

They were (and it's sad to say that some still are) stuck in self-destructive and animalistic behaviors. We could not load them into spaceships, even if we had them, and bring them home as we knew they would try to destroy our home planet. Our comparison may sound harsh, but we want you to try and understand. You would not take a wild tiger from the jungle and let him live in your house. We could not raise the collective consciousness of the engineered human beings either. We had tried that, resulting in the overload of the nervous system that caused people to have psychotic breakdowns and episodes. It works the same today. Thus, your higher self-energy comes in intervals so your nervous system can handle it. Too much will cause an overload.

The only way we could save the humans was to give them access to knowledge. They could learn who they are and their past and thrive. Mystery schools supplied that. All our knowledge was carefully separated into levels or classes. Once you passed all the teachings and tests from one level, you could move on to the next. If you could not pass a test, you had to repeat it, even if it took a lifetime. Today, the mystery school curriculum is woven into your everyday life (if you applied for it, in soul form, before birth). There are lessons to be learned and tests to pass. We know you can do this.

Sharing knowledge with humans was also intended to reduce wars. When one rises from fear into unconditional love, one will not indulge in war, arguments, greed, etc.

The last important part about Egypt you need to know is that our goal was to leave as much information about ancient wisdom as possible. After we made contact with our extraterrestrial families on our home planets, many of us consciously chose to stay on Earth for thousands and thousands of years to come. We can see the future, even though we know it is simply a potential future, as the future can be altered. Nevertheless, we foresaw several possibilities for humanity. Based on that, we tailored our teachings and built megalithic structures that would withstand the test of time and work to trigger your soul memories to remember who you are. When the Annunaki deliberately altered and confused all languages, we left pictures since the eyes are the doorway to the soul. If you perceive what you see with your soul (your heart) instead of your mind, you will understand the meaning because you have already learned it in mystery schools.

ANIMAL SPIRITS

Deliberately, we left pictures of half human and half animal to remind you of your DNA. (ET and animal) In Egyptian drawings, you will perceive us with an animal's head and a human's body. We would like you to take a few minutes to figure out to which God, goddess, or deity you feel drawn to most. (Sekhem, Thoth, Horus, Ra, Seth, Isis, Hathor, Anubis, etc.) Listen to your inner GPS; do not listen to your desire; simply listen to your soul.

Once you know your soul answer, you will know your animal DNA tribe. If you feel drawn to more than one, utilize both. This is how you interpret your animal DNA so you can work with it. For example, Sekhem used feline DNA to have a physical body that would function in the Earth's environment. Thus, she was gifted in positive aspects (like night vision, speed, strength, power, and protection of her young, etc.) and negative aspects (animal ferocity). Thoth used bird DNA (excellent physical navigation system, binocular vision, flying, prediction of natural disasters) and negative aspects (animal ferocity).

Do not stop yourself in Egypt; investigate Earth's history and figure out who you feel drawn to (who in history is depicted with animal body parts). Take the aspect of that animal and make it your totem animal. Imagine that you have this animal ability; because you do, they are just suppressed. Learn all about the positive aspects of this animal and learn to control the negative aspects. We have demonstrated these gifts to you through our appearances. We did not choose to look weird or funny to you but rather to show you these aspects so you can embrace who you are. Before adopting your alien abilities, you must understand all your Earthly abilities.

Today, you are all human beings. Some of you originated from animal life on Earth and were later upgraded by the Annunaki, mastering the mystery school. Despite this, you chose to remain with us to assist humanity through the challenging times ahead. We like to call you Earth-Seeds. You feel with humanity and take their burden upon your own shoulders. You feel your ancestors came from the stars but are still determining if you did. Your birthright is to know that your parents were extraterrestrials; therefore, you are also one. You possess abilities they have. You earned it.

Some of you are us, Pleiadians, Sirians, Andromedians, Orionians, etc. We like to call you Star-Seeds. You know who you are. Your heart is beating fast in recognition that you are an extraterrestrial being living in the human body who can remember living on other planets before your life here on Earth. You are an ascended master living in a human body. Now, take a deep breath, and remember, one is not better than the other. Earth-Seed or Star-Seed these are just names and words. We are all equal, no matter where you came from. Your actions are what matters, not the words that you call yourselves. If your soul sings the song of unconditional love, we are all brothers and sisters of one family.

PART 2 – THE PATH OF DARK

Mesopotamia became a homeland for the Sons of Belial. Earth was always accessible to explore, so some of them had moved there a few thousand years before the destruction of Atlantis. Their main purpose for this was to work on genetic projects in secret since such was illegal in Atlantis.

The Sons of Belial are more commonly known as the Annunaki. The Annunaki were extraterrestrials from almost all star nations that joined the Earth project. Not all the Annunaki had evil intentions when moving to Mesopotamia. Some extraterrestrials who were invited to this territory were very positive. They were spiritual and on the Path of Light and had a bright vision for the future of Earth. They were scientists, engineers, doctors, etc. They were fascinated with the opportunity to partake in genetic experiments. Unfortunately, many of them were coaxed into believing that all of the genetic experiments they worked on were approved by the Council of Light.

The Annunaki were the creators of the Sumerian civilization. Human beings lived among Annunaki as slaves. At the beginning of the Sumerian civilization, only a few Annunaki desired ultimate power and control. These few secretly planned the massive takeover that occurred thousands of years later. In the

154

overall scheme of things, they were not much different from some humans today. For comprehension, we call this the Path of Dark because they had chosen to follow the ego instead of the soul.

THE CREATION OF HUMANS

The Annunaki were dissatisfied because their plan to create human slaves did not receive the support they expected. As a result, they moved to Mesopotamia to secretly conduct their own experiments without the knowledge of the Council of Light. The human slaves were meant to be temporary, and the Annunaki intended to end the project once the slaves were no longer needed. Many who initially assisted in the genetic engineering experiments were deceived, as they genuinely believed that the Council of Light had finally agreed to their request.

The first attempts at genetically engineering humans were tremendous failures, most ending with odd-looking creatures such as half-animal and half-human. Neither extraterrestrial nor primate DNA was used for this type of experiment. The creatures were different, unpredictable, and dangerous. They became bitter and wild because they belonged nowhere. They were not extraterrestrials, and they were not animals either.

The Annunaki scientist had a breakthrough when studying primitive primates. Primitive primate families were native to Earth and already thriving. Annunaki scientists studied their behavior and routines. Once again, the scientists and genetic engineers who initially worked on this project had no intentional evil plans. Many of them were acclaimed doctors from faraway star nations such as Virgo. The opportunity to study primates and speed up their evolution fascinated them. They were told this was just a controlled project with the necessary clearance. All subjects would be terminated in the end. Primates were chosen due to their genetic makeup in comparison to extraterrestrials. They had the predicted growth of intelligence with the ability to listen and understand and perform and follow given tasks.

The scientists informed the head of the Annunaki that they would need to infuse extraterrestrial DNA into their primates to speed up their evolution. First, they used Annunaki DNA. However, it malfunctioned since their animal energy was more vital than the star's energy (because of their egos - animal component of DNA). Instead of having mellow and obedient slaves, they created intelligent, aggressive, and furious ones. These beings were terminated entirely. Later on, the Annunaki collectively determined that what they needed for their experiment to be successful was DNA from a Surrogate God. They required the combined stellar energy from the unadulterated Surrogate God deposition. It was pure.

As you can easily imagine, the Annunaki stole samples of the DNA from the Surrogate God and infused primates with it. To remind you, the Surrogate God crystal held OUR star collective energy.

For example, it is like someone stealing human sperm and eggs from a fertility bank and creating thousands, if not millions, of human babies without your consent.

The Annunaki successfully accomplished their plan of creating human slaves. Humans have become more intelligent faster than initially expected.

ULTIMATE CONTROL

What is the best tool for controlling or manipulating anyone? Fear! Human slaves were kept in a state of fear so that they were easier to maintain. Survival was embedded as a critical factor in their basic programming. Fear ensured survival.

In the beginning, humans were not allowed to reproduce. The Annunaki ensured this by disconnecting this basic animal function during the genetic engineering. As a reward for their obedience, doing the hard work they were supposed to, mining the gold, etc., the Annunaki permitted them to indulge in behaviors that would become addictive, such as sex, food, drugs, etc. Once someone is addicted to something, they will eventually be under the control of their supplier.

After a while, the Annunaki became tired of creating new bodies, so they gave humans the "gift" of reproduction. If you think it was a gift from the heart, think again. Allowing them to reproduce gave the Annunaki more power and control. It is an animal instinct to want to reproduce. Human slaves felt like gods when they were given this privilege because, until then, only gods could reproduce among each other.

Before they gave the humans this gift, the humans, collectively, had to plead allegiance to the Annunaki. This meant that everyone "born" as a human would be slaves to the Annunaki and would belong to them forever and ever. The Annunaki used fear tactics to diminish the lure that freedom possessed.

Humans believed that creating new life would turn them into gods. They literally signed their souls away to the Annunaki for this purpose. They willingly swore on their contracts with their blood. This was the time in which blood magic was born. The whole human slave race (which was tiny at the moment of the collective oath) was beholden to the Annunaki. Blood carries the program that the ego uses to protect your survival and possible reproduction. Blood is life, blood is passion, blood is connection, blood is energy, and blood is family. You can provoke intense pleasure or fear by directly introducing them into the bloodstream or food.

Everything you consume enters the bloodstream. Your blood is potent. Although the human race was enslaved to the Annunaki and further controlled through blood contracts, you still possessed free will and could regain your freedom.

Since that day, every soul born into a physical body is controlled through fear so that they can pass it on to the next generation.

Humans were tricked into a false belief regarding reproduction. Instead of becoming god-like, humanity became enslaved for thousands and thousands of years. Humans became puppets for the dark side.

The Sumerian civilization was the cradle of humanity. It was also the cradle of fear, control, and manipulation. This is still in effect today.

LANGUAGE

The fall of the Tower of Babel in ancient Sumer marked the timeline in which the universal language was intentionally manipulated and scrambled into many different languages. This was done so that humans could not freely communicate with one another. Eventually, some intelligent humans realized that natural reproduction did not make them god-like. While humans continued their search to become god-like, a few Annunaki, who were never power-hungry in the first place, started to realize that they had been misled in creating the humans. They felt terrible for the suffering they bestowed upon the humans by genetically engineering them, so they began guiding the humans to the knowledge that humans were made of extraterrestrial DNA. Thus, humans could be like those whom they worshiped and worked for. At that time, the knowledge of an actual God was significantly suppressed. It was suppressed so that the Annunaki could act like gods without human slaves trying to intervene.

Tension between the Annunaki gods escalated. Half wanted to free the slaves, while the other half desired superior control.

Many humans were evolving quickly with the newly learned knowledge from the good Annunaki. This frightened the Annunaki, who wanted to be in control. They could foresee losing their precious control if they did not do something soon. There is nothing more frightening for a bully than losing control. Those Annunaki who wanted to continue being in control decided to halt communication by confusing the primary language at the fall of the Tower of Babel.

Notice that many languages today are composed of letters instead of numbers or geometric shapes. Combining at least two letters from the same language will create syllables. From syllables, you can make words. You express your feelings, needs, and desires with words. This results in communication. The

Annunaki wanted obedient servants, not deaf or mute ones. They believed that by scrambling the language, the servants would be unable to communicate with one another and would conspire against them.

Imagine all existing letters and syllables as pieces to a big puzzle. Multiply this by three so that you have three big puzzles. Now, mix all the pieces from all three puzzles together in one big box and shake the box well. Now, randomly separate all the pieces into seven piles. Here, you have the start of the seven original human languages. As humanity evolved, more languages were developed.

The Annunaki used frequency to rapidly alter language, rewiring neural pathways in the brain and causing a concussion that blocked previous memories within minutes. We have previously mentioned the Lyrans and their genetic experiments. We would like to share an excerpt from the book "Activate Your Cosmic DNA: Discover Your Starseed Family from the Pleiades, Sirius, Andromeda, Centaurus, Epsilon Eridani, and Lyra," which further explains the technology they used.

"On Lyra, we lived very long lives. As a Lyran, you could control your body and what your life would look like. Upon your birth on Lyra, you will fully understand your previous lives. You can easily access information in your Akashic Record through your conscious mind. We, Lyrans, could also tamper with our consciousness. This would be done for varying reasons. For example, if you dedicate a certain amount of time to particular research, such as solar energy, you could temporarily alter your conscious mind and neurological energy pathways (receivers of the information) to receive only that information related to solar energy. This would give you a greater focus on a particular topic, solar energy, in this example. While consciously avoiding other distractions, your work regarding solar energy research would do very well. To further explain this, imagine a child prodigy who was born with autism. He could be a genius in one subject while lacking skills in others. We can do this consciously by altering neurological pathways within the brain and reversing them back and forth. This knowledge allowed us to play God on Earth. We were masters in the genetic and bioengineering fields."

With this knowledge and technology, the Annunaki blocked the memory of the Universal language, and humanity entered a deep hypnotic state.

We want you to notice that numbers, geometric shapes, and colors are part of the original universal language. They are part of the Language of Light that our ancient ancestors understood and spoke. Note that mathematical equations are valid all over the world. The answer is always the same; it does not matter what language you speak. Numbers are always accurate. God created this Universe in a mathematical pattern. No one could scramble that. It would totally destroy your Universe if it were scrambled. Therefore, you do have part of the original language. This is why mathematicians like Pythagoras kept this brilliant language alive. There is a lot of spiritual meaning behind formulas. This is also why repeating numbers are unique, as they have spiritual messages.

The Annunaki also could not take away your ability to see. Blind men make poor slaves. The eyes are the doorway to your soul, and your soul has memories. They are encoded within your DNA. When you look at ancient paintings, structures, and buildings, they remind you of your past. We built them with the intention that they might speak to your soul so that you can remember who you are. All you have to do is trust yourself and your feelings.

LEARNING TO DECODE THE UNIVERSAL LANGUAGE OF NUMBERS

You can decode the language of numbers in your everyday life. This will allow you to start consciously understanding the Language of Light. Notice what you are thinking about when a specific pattern of numbers appears in your life. It is the Universe giving you answers to your questions.

We are teaching you to read the language of numbers to be your own individual instead of following someone's lead or control. When you start learning, the number of repeating numbers does not matter; only the number does (1, 2, 3, etc). Once you become fluent in your interpretations, you can add numbers together to discover another level of meaning. For example, if you see 111 (1+1+1=3), you will work with the number 1 (your solid base). After understanding the essential meaning, you will later add the meaning of the number 3 to your original message (which will add additional information). It is the same as if you were learning to speak any language. First, you start with simple sentences of verbs and nouns and then add adjectives.

Below, we will use triple digits because the mind registers repeating numbers as a pattern. Once you see this pattern and consciously acknowledge it, you will begin to recognize that it holds secret messages for you.

The number 111 represents a new beginning, a fresh start. Pay attention to your plans. What changes are you considering? Are you thinking about switching jobs, writing a book, joining a gym, etc.? 111 is a sign that your new endeavor will bring positive change.

The number 222 represents the present moment, duality, choices, and two lines that can make a circle. The number 2 represents two parts of your ego (the victim and bully), two parts of your soul (past and future), and two parts of you (creative and destructive). The choice is always yours regarding which one you will embrace.

When you see the number 2, pay attention to your present thoughts. Recalling what you were thinking when you noticed the number is essential. Most likely, it was an idea that needed a decision. Do not procrastinate; make a decision from your heart and act upon it. The number 2 is not about planning but staying in the moment and dealing with everything that comes now."

The number 333 represents awareness and acts as a catalyst, with three lines creating a triangle. It symbolizes the connection between the past, present, and future. When you notice this number, pay attention to any significant events happening in your life and consider how these events are influenced by your past, present, and future. Is there anything from your past or past that you need to heal for these events to succeed? For instance, if you're getting married, starting a new business, etc., and keep seeing 333 everywhere, is there anything from the past that needs healing to ensure a spectacular future?

When you see the number 3, focus on healing your past and setting goals for the future while being consciously present in the moment. Once you've addressed issues from your past, your future self can more easily guide you in creating your desired future. Remember, working consciously in the present moment is the catalyst that the number 3 represents.

The number 444 represents spiritual and physical abundance, depending on what you thought about when you saw the number 4. For example, if you worry about your finances and want to enroll in a course or school but are still determining how you can afford it or if this will help you become abundant, seeing the number 4 is a good sign. This is your affirmation that your actions will be plentiful. Number 4 applies not only to finances but also to your collective abundance. When pondering if your actions will be abundant, seeing the number 4 is your yes answer. Remember that you need to practice to make good choices from the heart.

The number 555 symbolizes transformation. It signifies a significant change, presenting an opportunity to alter your patterns, behaviors, and mindset for the better. It may indicate that you are about to experience a period of inner turmoil, during which you are prepared to let go of your old self and embrace a new one. Practice feeling secure, align yourself with the Universe and trust your higher self to lead you.

The number 666 represents a conscious cooperation between your ego and your soul. It shows you the truth if you are ready to see it. Six is a number of duality, as it can be split into two equal parts, two triangles. Six is a number in which you can consciously recognize deception or be unconsciously deceived. Some say six is evil because they do not want you to find the truth.

When you see the number 6, it means you are aligning with your higher self. It's essential to develop and trust your intuition. For instance, if you have a new boss and keep seeing the number 6, it could be a warning sign that you need to know something about the new boss. You need to figure out what it is. Trust that you can see the truth and ask your guides for assistance. Your guides may show you that your new boss is just as nervous as you are about the changes, or they may show you that the new boss is driven by ego. By knowing the truth, you can take the right actions toward your success.

The number 777 represents the alignment between your spiritual and physical body. There are seven main chakras, seven Sisters of Pleiades, and seven days a week. When you see the number 7, you align yourself with your life mission physically and spiritually. Remember what you were thinking about when you saw the number 7, as it may give you a good glimpse into your life mission.

The number 888 symbolizes infinity and the potential for personal transformation. It also represents the unconditional love of God and abundance. The number 8 reminds you that you are deeply loved and that your life has endless possibilities. It invites you to explore this realm of potential.

The number 999 signifies the end of a cycle. This is an opportunity to bring closure to a pattern or phase in your life so you don't have to revisit it. Take a moment to reflect on what is coming to an end in your life, whether it's a project, a move, a relationship, or a job. Use this time to review your life, let go of past grievances, and send love to everyone involved. Look ahead and set new goals for a fresh start in a higher vibration cycle.

THE BIG FLOOD

Life after Atlantis has always been different from during the Atlantis period. Star beings experienced separation from each other, with some groups isolating themselves completely. We all focused on work that was important to us. Preserving knowledge for future generations was the main task for those on the Path of Light.

Restoring the intergalactic communication and transportation systems lost after Atlantis's destruction took considerable time. When the Council of Light discovered what was happening on Earth, they were highly displeased. They immediately ordered the complete evacuation of all extraterrestrials from Earth and the full termination of the genetically evolved human life project.

The Council of Light considered destroying the whole Earth, including all its extraterrestrials, if their decision was not obeyed. They spoke of Maldek, its destruction, and the possibility that Earth could be next. It may sound harsh, but even the Council of Light has another authority they must answer to above them. It was against the law to speed up the evolution of God's creations. Every action has a reaction. Evolving life on Earth could be either beneficial or destructive toward the rest of the Universe.

Extraterrestrials on the Path of Light pleaded with the Council of Light to save the human race and give them a fair chance to evolve in the future. After all, it was our collective mistake to use Earth for these experiments.

After a long delegation process with the Council of Light, we reached a compromise. A great cleansing (Big Flood) would take place while humans would be given a fair chance to survive and thrive under close monitoring from another planet, with the Council of Light keeping tabs on the operation.

It was agreed that if humans could fulfill the path of ascension as separate individuals, in groups, or collectively, they could join us in our home world. They would be welcomed as equal beings of love and light.

This is the beginning of The Game of Life because that is what it became. Imagine a board game with seven main territories influenced by different extraterrestrial families from other realms. We are awaiting answers to questions such as: "Who will win? What will you embrace, the star-being DNA or the animal DNA? Will your psyche allow you to accept, forgive, and embrace unconditional love? Can you handle the truth? Or will you succumb to the dark side?"

As you probably already know from ancient texts, the Big Flood historically marks a time when all extraterrestrials left Earth's surface. We made a deal with the Council of Light: no gods (extraterrestrials) would walk or live among humans. Extraterrestrials would not show themselves to the human race to ensure that humans would not worship fake gods. Humans have a chance to find the true god within them.

We were allowed to occupy the inner Earth to supervise. The main objective was to take care of the Earth and the Surrogate God crystal since our DNA had to stay anchored to the crystal so humans could survive. Without the energy of the Surrogate God crystal, the life of the human race would cease to exist because the soul energy in the humans could not survive on Earth for a long time without a bond to the physical realm. You may wonder, "Why not destroy the crystal and free all these souls"? The answer could be more pleasing. If the crystal gets destroyed before the souls graduate into higher realms, the souls who are not evolved will be trapped in levels of the lower dimensions. They would be stuck among entities like those who entered the Earth realm when the dimensions had been ripped open after the destruction of Atlantis.

Since the biblical Big Flood, we can only assist you in bringing knowledge to humanity by becoming your guide, speaking through or incarnating into a human body, and becoming a soul teacher.

Remember the seven territories? Now start connecting all your knowledge of the so-called "god" appearing to special humans, yet never revealing his identity, advising them to only follow one god and not to listen to another god, or significant destruction will follow. The Game of Life has to have balance, and since Earth is a place of duality, the Council of Light gave rights to darkness and light to play on Earth because they are "twin flames"! The only way to heal is to unite. One is equal. The only way to find the path home is through knowledge and healing of your soul-mind consciousness.

Incarnation in the human body has its own pros and cons. Light beings do not always enjoy living in the human body. We have to follow strict rules. Since the Big Flood, we can only incarnate in the human bodies that the Annunaki had genetically engineered. The human body has a limited life span; you cannot remember previous incarnations because your soul must cross the River of Forgetfulness before birth. The physical body is dominated by animal DNA. It is often raised within societies created by humans, with rules made by humans that may harm and damage the soul.

We consider you, our brothers, and sisters, all of you who resonate with our message and frequency, who took a leap of faith and incarnated on Earth to assist humanity as the bravest souls in the Galaxy!

You are HEROS! We are here to bathe you in unconditional love.

For the thousands of years that you have existed on Earth, you have been tortured, abused, and killed in many lifetimes. This is because you believe in assisting the human race in embracing the knowledge that they are divine children of God. We are here to illuminate your path on your game board so that you can see the golden staircase in the shape of the Fibonacci spiral that will lead you to the finish line.

Lastly, when you ascend, the characteristics brought on by your animal DNA will be tamed. Each of you will be a marvelous addition to extraterrestrial life. Mystery schools were designed to help you reach ascension. The Mayan experiment proved that these schools can be successful.

Kara – Akashic Record

This passage will explain how even those who have chosen the Path of Light could end on the Path of Dark.

Before the Earth realm caused Kara's spirit to break down, she used to be a joyful Pleiadian being, believing that everyone could change if they experienced the unconditional love of God. Her soul desperately wanted her to remember this so that she could embody this belief once again and spread love and light with others in her Earth life. Kara was a Pleiadian being who lived on the planet Electra. Before coming to Earth, she had no experience with low-vibration energies. Her soul was gentle and sweet. She consciously vibrated with the frequency of unconditional love. She was deeply connected to nature. She truly believed that everything was good. She trusted everyone and believed everyone.

Kara arrived on Earth during the time of Atlantis. She was a healer. She practiced healing techniques and herbal medicine and soul-developed her healing abilities while in Earth's realm. It is a Pleiadian's gift to be able to heal the soul. One of her missions in Atlantis was to assist beings caring for plants and trees. Some plants and trees from various planets in the Universe were brought to Earth to create lovely reminders of our homes. Many plants were used to make medicine for extraterrestrials.

Planet Electra is known for its healing trees and enchanted beings, such as elves and fairies, that live within its forests. When Kara came to Earth, she often met with fairies, dragons, elves, and various other benevolent beings of light. She knew how to get into the inner Earth. Unfortunately, about halfway through Atlantis, these enchanted beings became massively hunted (because of their unique energy) by other star beings whose egos became possessed.

When Kara arrived in Atlantis, genetic modification was in full gear and went unquestioned by new incoming beings. Her animal DNA was fish/amphibian.

(Please note that we did not use primate DNA in the original project to alter our extraterrestrial bodies. Primate DNA was used later to create humans as you know them today.)

About two thousand years before the destruction of Atlantis, Kara was invited to move to Mesopotamia (because of her unique fish/amphibian DNA). Her move was based on work choices, much like today's work-related relocation decisions. She was deciding to move to either Egypt or Sumer. The Annunaki persuaded her to move to Sumer by telling her that she was much more needed there, and many suffered from the side effects of genetic experiments. She took that path to be of service to others there. She had no idea what would happen to her, nor would she listen to others when they suggested she go to Egypt instead. She felt she had to go to Sumer to help those in need.

She sensed it would be a difficult journey, so secretly, she stayed connected with those in Egypt. This helped her keep her energy vibrant while sharing knowledge with those who sought it. Her soul's healing mission was to bring an understanding of the human ego to others so that they could evolve and find their soul power.

Living among the Annunaki caused Kara to witness some very dark events. One of them that we sensed during the session was her knowledge of the sexual abuse of humans. Some of the Annunaki used sex as a tool of power as well as a tool of fear. Kara spoke up against these acts and was accused of betraying the Annunaki. Most Annunaki wanted superior power; you were either with or against them. She was demoted from her god-like position and sent to live among the humans. Unfortunately, humans also were not kind to her. She was mistreated because she was different. She was raped and abused. Many others like her disagreed with the Annunaki and could not escape in time. She passed away in a violent death.

Her soul remembered living in Sumer. She remembered seeing the Annunaki's obscene sexual rituals, being scared of the Annunaki gods, and fearing the humans. Her soul was in shock; she could not understand how those she trusted and loved could do such horrible things to her. This was her original Earth soul wound. Her soul was literally screaming, "Why did I come here?"

CINDY

When I read for Cindy (Kara), her soul could not remember the essence of her Pleiadian being. She was unconsciously afraid she was terrible inside. Her soul felt unworthy to the point where she could not utilize her abilities because she believed she could possibly harm someone. This was just one false soul memory from her life among the Annunaki. She harmed no one.

Cindy shared that she tried to study spirituality and different energy methods. What was exciting in the beginning became meaningless later. Her human ego kept discouraging her from embracing her natural ability because of the belief that her soul could not withstand such levels of suffering again. Of course, the ego does not know that we do not have to repeat the past if we are brave enough to move forward. Pleiadians shared soul-healing exercises with Cindy and filled her with unconditional love so that she could forgive everyone and allow her soul to shine again.

SOUL HEALING

1. Accept your failure in Atlantis or in the Earth project. (We all failed at some time in history.)

Allow yourself to accept failure (even making poor decisions); it is fine, as it was in the past. How long will you punish yourself for it? You have already been forgiven. All you have to do is to forgive yourself and others.

If you feel in your heart that you are a star being living in a human body, look into a mirror, look deep into your eyes, and speak to your soul. Acknowledge that you are thousands, if not millions, of years old. Accept that you are an extraterrestrial living in a human body. Tell yourself that you are ready to remember who you indeed are. Ask your higher self to assist you on your journey.

2. Revoke the Annunaki Oath

Repeat out loud: *"By the power of my free soul will, I renounce the oath of allegiance I swore to the Annunaki and all others who are restricting me of my free will. I claim my soul power back. The blood circulating in my veins belongs to my body. My body is a vessel for my higher self. I am canceling all blood contracts made in my past and taking back full control of my destiny."*

3. Fill yourself with unconditional love

Repeat out loud: *"I call upon the highest energy of the Source/God to connect with me and my higher self, to fill me with unconditional love. I welcome unconditional love. Unconditional love is filling my whole body. I am sending unconditional love from inner core of my being into my auric field. If any negative energy or entity is attached to me, I am un-inviting you from my body and energy field. I am filling you with unconditional love and asking the family of light to return you back home."*

Express your gratitude and continue with your day. The key is to be able to ask for unconditional love and physically feel the unconditional love flowing into your body from head to toe. You will feel it if you believe you are connected to universal love. It may take a little practice, but it is not much different than when you see a lemon and can sense how sour it tastes without tasting it. With unconditional love, it works similarly. If you believe in it, you will feel it. Remember that unconditional love is the highest energy that heals. It is the essence of your being that others want you to forget

CHAPTER 9

THE BIRTH AND DEATH
OF JESUS CHRIST

Thousands of years have passed since the destruction of Atlantis, and you have several incarnations under your belt. Some were great, some were horrifying. Then, the highly anticipated time of significant change finally arrived. The birth of Jesus Christ. It is not relevant whether you agree or disagree that the son of God walked the Earth. However, realizing this was a significant time in your history, marking your second major soul wound, is proper. The life and death of Jesus Christ prompted the formation of several religions that sadly were (and still are) made to control humanity in the name of God and of Jesus instead of freeing them. An event that was divinely planned by the Pleiadians to eliminate fear and replace it with unconditional love took a terrible turn.

DESCENDANTS OF THE ATLANTEAN TRIBE

The ancient Atlantean tribe and the Children of Law of One kept their energy, knowledge, and traditions secretly alive to pass them from generation to generation. Life after the Big Flood was difficult. We cannot use sophisticated technology to assist humanity anymore. Spiritual and physical growth slowed down, and we had to settle into the natural evolution of life.

People were separated by languages, money, beliefs, fear, love, and hate. The physical body operated on the program of 3D survival and possible reproduction as designed. All extraterrestrials who desired to live on Earth had to be born into a human body, which (as you already know) was initially engineered by the Annunaki.

When incarnating into the human body, we followed secret spiritual teachings and practices to maintain our energy. We also practiced conscious conception to retain as many memories as possible, which was quite effective. In this practice, we connected with families that shared our energy vibrations and supported our missions.

We attended mysterious schools where the curriculum emphasized soul growth and understanding the ego, helping us transcend our animal DNA's limitations. This was intended to enable souls to move beyond the duality of the Earth realm and reunite with their soul families in the Universe. We taught others how to walk on the Path of Light and left behind numerous ancient documents and energy trails for others to follow.

Over time, there were fewer masters, mystery school teachers, and believers because we only had stories and teachings to pass on. Anything extraordinary had to be kept secret; otherwise, you could be stoned to death by those controlled by fear.

The male ego energy grew in superiority. Some became tempted by the dark side and left. We all missed our life in Atlantis and our home in the Universe. At times, suffering felt unbearable, as it is for you today. We kept our lives simplistic. Several independent female tribes were formed to protect territories and knowledge. Female energy is more challenging to corrupt, so we trusted divine guidance. We let our sisters guide us through some very dark times. We will share that males living in our tribes healed their egos and were in harmony with female leaders. Males and females of the Children of the Law of One were united in heart and mind and were bonded by unconditional love. We turned to nature, stayed connected with those living in the inner Earth, did not embrace animal or human sacrifices, and kept our bodies and souls as pure as possible. We, the Pleiadians (and many others), stay behind to walk beside you on Earth as your brothers and sisters.

Through our intuition and telepathy, we were connected with our soul families in the Universe, similar to how you are connected with us, the Pleiadians, by listening to our energy transmissions translated into words you can understand. During that time, we were instructed to be frequency holders, to write down all knowledge, and to preserve it for future generations. We were advised to wait patiently for a time that would be favorable to all of us.

THE SONS OF BELIAL

The Sons of Belials were also incarnate on Earth; they had their own prophets. As you see, it became a game, a Game of Life. Who would win? The Dark or Light? They felt they had invested much in humanity, so why not try to gain ultimate control? Understand that the ego takes control while love gives freedom.

We will remind you of the "basic rules" given. No extraterrestrial could visibly interfere with humanity. We could walk with you in a human body (we have to incarnate for that) or make you a prophet to channel our messages. Thus, the Council of Light would only interfere (not even today) if human actions were to threaten extraterrestrial life in the Universe.

THE ESSENES

The names of spiritual groups are irrelevant to us, but they are to you as they help you vaguely identify who you are and who you were during that period to heal your soul wounds.

Several of you remember your past life as Essenes. Naturally, you might wonder if you were Jesus Christ, Mary Magdalena, Anna, or one of the disciples, We. Stop you right here. Your soul does not care what name or identity it had while incarnated on Earth. Your soul cares about the mission it had and still has today. It is the ego who wants to feel superior. It can convince itself that you have been an essential player in your Earth's history, so it can keep you trapped in the game. We are trying to tell you that it does not matter who you were back then. What matters is who you do today. What actions will you take to serve humanity, and what kind of energy trail will you leave behind for others to follow?

The Essenes community began as a group of people deeply connected to the essence of their being and were pure in their souls. They could easily follow the accession path, yet they decided to stay. They were descendants of the ancient Atlanteans, the Children of the Law of One. They were called for by the God/Source and asked to step out of their hidden communities on Earth and into the spotlight of other existing religions and beliefs. This was so humans who were ready for change could easily find them. Planetary alignments supported this move similarly to how 2012 marked another window of opportunity for a significant change.

Some Essenes communities secretly lived an extended life span that covered several hundreds of years. They knew the secrets of immortality and had knowledge of the Rejuvenation Temple and herbal healing. They were also connected with the Mayans through beings living on the inner Earth. They never abused their ancient wisdom. They used it only to be in service. In a way, these people were walking libraries. It was required for them to live extended lifetimes. At the end of their natural life span, their soul accepted another mission and remained in the same physical body. This happened instead of going through another reincarnation and states of amnesia. They also documented history from the beginning of time, before the Sumerian civilization. Ancient texts will appear in the next few years to help you find the truth.

The Essenes (and later Gnostic) entered into history for the same reason as the pyramids did in Egypt, to help your soul recall its soul memories of energy that you have used. You may not remember everything, but you will most likely remember the food you ate, the clothes you wore, how you treated others in your community, and how you were treated. We hope you remember your respect for one another, mission, unconditional love, hope, faith, and visions of the New Earth. If you can remember fragments of this, you are remembering the essence of your being.

Jesus Christ

After the Essenes community was established and opened its doors to those willing to abide by its rules, which were based on unconditional love, many benevolent star beings were invited to return to Earth to help humanity during the expected shift. As star-seeded beings, many of you responded to this call and returned to Earth at that time. Like today, you faced the challenge of understanding the human psyche and physical body before fully remembering all your soul's knowledge.

We all wanted to help you and speed up your soul growth, so we arranged for the soul you call Jesus Christ to enter the earthly realm. The bodies and souls of Essene elders, Mary and Joseph, were trained to hold higher vibration frequencies and soul purity. This is how the soul of a Pleiadian being could enter Mary's womb without allowing the 4D energy of Heaven to enter and avoid crossing the River of Forgetfulness before coming to Earth. This event was perfectly planned. Mother Mary was not abducted by aliens or impregnated by God in her sleep. Mother Mary was a Pleiadian being living in a human body. She was a star-seeded being whose first life on Earth was in Lemuria.

Mother Mary was a cosmic mother. Since then, she has had several incarnations.

We had purposely chosen a male figure for Jesus Christ because males were dominant during that time. We believed that it would be easier to relate to a male public figure rather than a female, as she may have been killed during her first speech. However, we have also sent female beings, such as Mary Magdalene, who married Jesus and had children with him and eventually became even more essential in preserving the ancient Atlantean tribe throughout history.

Jesus Christ and Mary Magdalene walked on Earth among you to show you that you all are the same as them. They were raised in a community catering to their spiritual growth and physical needs. Remember that they did not need to train for a traditional job that would ensure their money, which humans believe is necessary for survival on Earth as it is used to obtain food and shelter. Since they were young, they were taught to understand the human part of them as well as the divine part of them. They were taught the same skills we are sharing with you. Their only advantage was being born in a community with this knowledge and the fact that they had no soul wounds. We would like to point out that Jesus Christ and Mary Magdalene were not predestined to marry, nor was their marriage arranged by others. They followed their human hearts and made the best of their life on Earth. There are many things we cannot or would not influence. Everyone has a free will. You can easily follow this path while healing your soul wounds and still be responsible for making choices.

Their primary sole purpose was to demonstrate that anyone could be like them. They showed that you are a child of God, made in the image of God, and God is within you. Your body is a temple for unconditional love, and your heart is the candle of your infinite light.

Essenes did not make themselves superior to anyone; they treated everyone equally. Several Essenes had the same abilities as Jesus, but you would never know if you walked beside them. They respected you for who you were and your choices, even if they were not in your best interests. They would never force you to change your beliefs or instill fear (or any kind of control). They would guide you to knowledge so that you could free yourself from the reality you were currently experiencing at that period. You are the creator of your life and your destiny.

YEAR ONE

The death of Jesus Christ was not planned, as some religious texts may tell you. The Sons of Belial felt highly threatened by the Essene's upcoming popularity; since humans truly believed that the son of God walked among men, they had to stop it.

The Sons of Belial were behind the creation of various religions, secret societies, and the crucifixion of Christ. They carefully planned it to ultimately control humanity. Every religion, belief, and spiritual practice on Earth carries part of the divine truth. Not all is a lie. However, when someone tells you that you must live your life a specific way, they are more than trying to control you. If someone tells you that bad things will happen to you for not following this or that, then that someone is trying to instill fear in you. Of course, this topic is debatable. We will share the rules set with unconditional love that the Essenes followed. You had a choice to follow the rules and live in the community or leave by your free will. You could follow your own rules, live where your heart desired, and yet be supported by them. It is the same as the Pleiadians will not demand that you all be vegetarians, vegans, or carnivores. You know that all three mentioned groups can channel us. We go to the ones with pure hearts and do not look at what you have in your stomach.

Now, back to our topic of the first year. When it became apparent that Jesus would be crucified, the Essenes made a collective plan to demonstrate unconditional love to humankind instead of hiding him (which they all could have quickly done). Jesus's soul was fully healed. He forgave everyone for everything they needed to be forgiven for, and he held everyone in the frequency of unconditional love. He did not suffer for the humans. He was not in pain for a long time. His soul was trained to astral project above his body and disconnect from physical pain. It lasted three days and three nights. Number three is the catalyst we mentioned throughout this book. The Essenes needed three days to create a wave of unconditional love around the Earth.

In those three days, everyone on the Path of Light sent unconditional love to Jesus Christ, who served as a torus of this energy, which flowed into the crystalline grid of Earth, connecting with the Surrogate God crystal, and through his body into the Pleiades and the whole Universe. Rainbow energy of unconditional love flowed for three days and three nights to cleanse and purify humanity. Deep inside us, we all desire to be loved, despite who we are, and so all souls who want or need love benefit from this rainbow energy. Those who were closed did not receive this energy. Energy works based on the law of free will.

The effect had been highly successful. What happened around the Earth was rather phenomenal. Finally, the heart of humanity came together (for one tiny moment because everyone needs love). Despite religion, faith, belief, race, economic group, and countries, they all agreed to start the first year in the calendar as we know it today. Of course, your historians have a logical explanation, but we have ours. The unconditional love held for three days by all willing souls marked the change of time. The death and resurrection of Jesus Christ gave humanity the chance for a new beginning. The Earth's core was beaming with unconditional love. Whether earth-seeded or star-seeded, humans received the soul calling to become unconditional love, frequency keepers, and crystal keepers. In each generation, a few are asked to pass on the torch of love and light to another generation. At this time, we ask all of you to become frequency keepers (and the protectors of love and light). This will not keep you stuck in the incarnation cycle because you can consciously disconnect from this job by the end of your natural life.

The Sons of Belial spun the story of Jesus Christ in a way that worked for them to control most of the population. Within the past 2,000 years, they had to devise a few more sinister scenarios to wipe away the smile we had in our hearts on that day.

ANCIENT ATLANTEAN RULES FOLLOWED BY THE ESSENES

The Trinity
1. Love, kindness, and compassion
2. Respect, discipline, and rules set with love
3. Teach by example, give space to experiment, and allow space for soul growth

Embrace unconditional love, respect others' choices, and teach by example.

Be kind to yourself and others, obey the discipline you created for a healthy body, mind, and soul, and give yourself space to honestly experiment with what is working for you and what is not.

Have compassion toward life, set rules with the energy of love to accomplish your goals, and allow yourself space for soul growth.

These simple yet effective rules were created with unconditional love toward your soul and could be applied to any aspect of your life. Whether it involves being a good parent, sister, brother, employee, or business owner, we like to follow these rules (and we are reminding you of them).

If these rules resonate with you, you will feel it in your heart. If not, we encourage you to search for what works uniquely for you.

Soul healing during this period is achieved by the pure realization that Jesus Christ was here to show you that you are like him, with each of you having his abilities. No one is more special. Each of you is your own healer and guru, and no one should be put on a pedestal to be worshiped. It does not matter who you specifically were in your past lives; it only matters who you are today.

Take a little time to go within and question your fear of religion, beliefs, and spiritual groups. Identify times when you felt controlled by them, by concerns about believing something would happen to you if you did not believe as they believed. Simply realize that those were just humans trying to have superior control over you, whether in this lifetime or past lifetimes. When you become conscious of it, the next step is to forgive. How long will you let all these fears and anger control you?

Forgive and step back into your soul power. Imagine you are part of the cosmic Christ consciousness walking on Earth. You all are Jesus Christ and Mary Magdalene. You all have divine masculine and feminine energies within. Stay humble and keep your ego in check.

CHAPTER 10

THE WISE WOMEN
AND THE WITCH TRIALS

"When you feel as if walking through a dark tunnel embraced by fear, stop for a moment, close your eyes, and take a deep breath. Know that your soul sisters, Hope and Faith, are always by your side. Hold their hands and let them guide you while walking through the darkness until you see the light again." ~ Pleiadians

Those on the Path of Light who were initiated in ancient Atlantean teachings knew that Jesus Christ did not die on a cross, but they could not reveal this truth to anyone as it would undo its intended effect.

We would like you to notice the messages hidden in numbers. We had 33 conscious years to raise Earth's energy level. The number three is a catalyst that bridges energy between the past, present, and future. The three days of unconditional love (for Earth and its inhabitants) allowed significant soul healing and opened doorways for a better future.

Another layer of this energy included the number 6. (3+3 =6). The number six brings consciousness into the physical and spiritual body. It guides you to make your own choices, whether they are creative or destructive. Six is a number that lets you consciously recognize deception if you are willing to see it.

In summary, the energy of this event set new GPS coordinates for the future and allowed you to either recognize deception or be deceived. Ultimately, it gave you the power to free yourself and live your truth.

After the crucifixion, the Sons of Belial scrambled to regain their control. They could not wipe out the memory of Jesus Christ, but they could use that same memory for their own purposes of ultimate control. They did that by glorifying Jesus Christ through religion and secret societies. Over thousands of years, they learned that:

- People need to believe in something to pursue what they think is happiness, and they (the Sons of Belial) could define happiness for them.

- The ego wants to feel in control.

- Superiority is something they would fight for under the name of God.

- Humans are gullible beings who can be fooled by cheap tricks.

- Since the beginning of time, the Sons of Belial have used human weaknesses and their addictions to control them.

They would use this knowledge to stop the Children of the Law of One. They would use the name of Jesus to control, kill, and destroy everyone on the Path of Light.

This created your third major soul wound between the 12th and 16th centuries, The witch trials.

MARY MAGDALENE

After Christ's crucifixion, certain people of the Essenes community, a close soul family, followed Mary Magdalene to Europe. She became the leader of their community. She held the frequency of the feminine divine energy (unconditional love) and was highly respected.

To outsiders, Mary Magdalene was expected to be a mourning widow, and the Essenes community was expected to be broken and too scared to practice anything.

They played their roles well; no one suspected that Mary Magdalena was pregnant, nor that Jesus Christ was resurrected. Once she moved to Europe, her secret mission started. She was well-trained and highly respected by all the secret surviving tribes of the Children of the Law of One. As an adept of the mystery school, she was asked to become the master teacher of the Wise Women (and men) who would eventually scatter and live in peaceful tribes all over Northern Europe. This was the beginning of what later would be known as the Knights Templar, Freemasons, and other secret societies.

They knew connecting enough souls to create another unconditional love catalyst would take the next few hundred years. In the meantime, they worked to preserve and record the ancient teachings as handed down to them. They copied many ancient scripts and saved them in places where they would be protected and shared with the world when the right time came. They wrote new books to record history, known as the Scripts of the Living Truth.

Ancient beings from the inner Earth assisted them with their knowledge and hid the books as much as possible. Slowly, keeping these connections alive became more complex and dangerous.

The Sons of Belial worked hard on their part. They corrupted the minds of many good people. Finding people outside the tiny communities you could fully trust became more challenging.

Poisoned thoughts, consisting of God's betrayal or his eventual betrayal of humans, were seeded in the minds of many.

THE WISE WOMEN

The time came and went, and by the twelfth century, the Wise Women communities quietly thrived in secluded parts of Northern Europe. Secretly, they kept teachings from the mystery school alive. Their knowledge spanned back to ancient Atlantis.

Many turned to the Wise Women when they became ill instead of consulting doctors. Wise Women would help them by providing inexpensive or free herbal remedies, whereas doctors would charge outrageous amounts of money while hardly fulfilling their promise of health. The most notable account of their rising popularity came about when people started to seek advice from the Wise Women on regular life issues such as love, abundance, happiness, etc. Their guidance was practical and lacked the fear that religions flourished from. More and more regular people sought them out for consultations.

Assisting someone as they rose out of fear into love always sent red flags to the dark side. This is how the Wise Women became visible on the dark side's radar, and the power struggle became inevitable.

With the newly extended demand for their light work, the Wise Women communities grew frustrated while waiting for the energy to be favorable enough to teach everyone the true God. They disliked the way religions used the name of God to control everyone. They were sick of their lies.

For the past twelve hundred years, they have protected ancient knowledge, passing it on from generation to generation. Among them lived a few who still used the ancient Atlantean techniques of extending one's life span for hundreds of years.

The primary rationale for extending one's lifespan was to become a Wisdom Keeper, also known as a living librarian. These individuals served humanity by preserving original knowledge through writing numerous books for future generations. They passed this knowledge on to the future and were dedicated to serving humanity at a soul level. To achieve "temporary immortality," one must have a clear soul purpose. This is the only acceptable way to prolong one's physical lifespan.

These individuals had to live in secrecy, and their existence slowly became a myth. It was dangerous for communities to shelter "immortals." The Sons of Belial were active in many churches and preached superiority. They carefully searched for indications that the Children of the Law of One were passing on their knowledge. If caught, punishments were gruesome.

Therefore, the Wise Woman adjusted their effort on how to keep knowledge alive. Instead of focusing on extending life spans, the Wise Women adopted the ancient Atlantean practice of preparing souls for Earth's journey before entering the woman's womb. This ensured that the soul's memory would remain with the baby as it matured into young adulthood and that the spiritual door would not close. These souls were assisted in developing their consciousness since early childhood to carry on their soul's mission. In their childhood, they were told stories about their ancient alien ancestors and of Master Thoth and others. Those who demonstrated a deep interest in spirituality were guided, in secrecy, to learn from ancient records. The books were skillfully hidden and hard to access; otherwise, they would be either burned or confiscated by the Sons of Belial if they were discovered. For this reason, it was safer to teach by word of mouth.

These times were frustrating for everyone. The council of the Wise Women wondered if they should follow God's guidance or take action to make changes on Earth.

Females were strong and participated in a few wars. The council of the Wise Women agreed that instead of fighting wars, it may be more beneficial to move out of their isolated hiding places, live among ordinary people, and teach those open to receiving their knowledge. Those who fell in love could marry out of their community if desired. This movement was because if a man fell in love with a Wise Woman, he would slowly change, allowing those around him to also change. One family at a time. They knew that love was the highest energy, and that unconditional love would conquer all evil.

The opposition's agenda was robust. Sons of Belial were brainwashing men to believe that they had superior power and that women were only good at bearing children, taking care of their men, doing the household chores, etc.

THE WITCH HUNT

The Sons of Belial became threatened once more.
More and more people began searching for these Wise
Women. Sickness does not discriminate between the
rich and the poor; it strikes when you least expect it.
The Wise Women could have looked away while
suffering but chose to help instead. Even men were
willing to listen to the women who cured them of their
painful sicknesses. They mended broken bones, healed
shattered souls, brought wisdom, and reminded them of
hope and faith. Fear was going down on the collective
barometer, and unconditional love was rising.

The Sons of Belial needed to devise a way to
prevent and stop this for good. They were crafty, dark
beings. They knew that when their ancestors crucified
Jesus, Jesus transcended fear and physical pain to create
the unconditional love catalyst on Earth. They guessed
that some of these Wise Women had the same training.
Thus, the plan to eliminate them had to extend beyond
death to ensure their removal. They debated and argued
until they devised a frightful scenario for the light souls.

The Wise Women would be called witches. Their
healing work would be called witchcraft and the work
of the devil. Anyone accused of witchcraft would be
sentenced, by officials, to death.

They were tortured, raped, and their children and
loved ones were killed in front of them. We do not like
to be graphic, but in your soul, you may remember

being forced to watch these horrifying scenes while feeling hopeless and angry. Angry with yourself, with your community, and with God. How could something like this be happening? Your soul still holds such trauma from those days that many of you are still deathly afraid to open this forbidden door of knowledge to your own soul power.

THE SOUL CAVE

The eyes are the doorway to the soul. During each incarnation, the soul records all major soul wounds and stores them in the Soul Cave. If soul wounds are not healed during the particular lifetime in which they occurred, they will manifest as blockages in the next lifetime and continue until one is strong enough to look into the past and heal them.

The Sons of Belial knew this, so they used it to their advantage. Through experience, they found that if they tortured you personally, you might just simply embrace it and accept it like Jesus did. However, if they were to have you witness the physical and emotional torture of your loved ones and make you believe that their pain is due to your actions, this would shatter and break you. Eventually, you would fall into despair, thinking it was entirely your fault. You would start believing that being a Wise Woman or a healer was its own curse.

The Sons of Belial knew that if you (as Wise Women or Wise Men) witnessed your child die in a slow, brutal, and excruciating way and you were not able to save that child, you would blame yourself and bring this information into your Soul Cave. You would tell your soul to NEVER use your abilities again because it resulted in the death of someone you dearly loved. This information would override all urges to assist others, to be a healer, or to be a wise one ever again since you would believe that your family might suffer if you do.

The Soul Cave is your soul's record-keeping system used to store only information from all your lives here on Earth, unlike your Akashic Record, which stores information from all your lives throughout the Universe. When the Surrogate God crystal was created in the inner Earth to anchor your soul energy, your higher self has created your Soul Cave to keep track of each life. It was an action-reaction process. This is the perfect example of duality, where two components work together to achieve unity one day. The Soul Cave's purpose is to help you remember what you need to heal in your soul before you can disconnect your anchor from the Surrogate God crystal. What happens on the Earth has to be healed on Earth before you can leave the incarnation cycle and return home.

Each Earth's life is represented by a crystal. Only you have access to your cave, no one else. Thus, the Sons of Belial did not have entry to this information in your Soul Cave. However, they could torture you so you would (by your own free will) restrict your own abilities and stop pursuing the Path of Light to change the world.

Your soul keeps its own records for future incarnations, and when you are ready to reincarnate again, it sends this information to your ego. Your ego will apply that program to your "survival manual" of "what not to do." In other words, it will try to prevent you from repeating this kind of life (exercising your abilities) again since it caused your soul suffering in the past.

The soul cannot be destroyed, but it can enter a state of amnesia, refusing to cooperate with anyone or anything (even God). It would just wander through a space, lost and without any direction. There is a particular unit that assists these souls and investigates the details of how this happened. No beings (dark or light) want to be found responsible for lost souls, as what follows is neither pretty nor a topic for this book. If you read this, your soul most likely has deep wounds but is not lost.

THE WAR BETWEEN THE DARK AND THE LIGHT

During the time of the witch hunts, many of you rushed through incarnations and had anywhere between 3-5 lifetimes (some of you more), which ended by being burned, drowned, disfigured, beheaded, etc. After each death, you hurried to return to help your community and keep the Path of Light alive. You hoped and prayed that you would learn something to help stop this horrid genocide of the souls who were on the Path of the Light. This, indeed, was the war between the Dark and the Light. As we mentioned, the purpose of this cruel treatment was so that beings of light would ultimately stop using their power and become stagnant.

The Sons of Belial hid within religious houses created to gain superior power over humankind and peacefully rule the men of Earth with the sword of fear. In their dark minds, no light beings would challenge them anymore.

THE FIGHT IS ON

The Wise Women would not give up. They were fighters and survivors. Think of the brave female warriors of the Amazon. Once inquisitors established their position against them and brutally killed them and their families in the name of God, it became personal. They decided to take fate into their own hands and give each other hope.

They were so angry and desperate to save their own kind they did not ask God for guidance. They thought that God would not understand the pain and suffering they were enduring. They were desperate and raged for revenge. Since Ancient Atlantis, they kept coming back and reincarnating on Earth. They had a choice to leave and go home, but instead, they decided to stay and teach humanity, help them evolve, and keep the frequency of Love and Light strong.

In all those years, they continued to encourage one another to keep going, but now, with the inquisitions and the witch hunts, it seemed that the spiritual growth of humanity would never happen. They grew tired and impatient. They were tired of hiding, tired of the unfairness, tired of being hunted, and tired of the murders of innocent people, all in the name of God. Were they destined to be killed because they would not obediently and blindly listen to religious men? Men who twisted ancient history and rewrote the Bible several times for no other reason than to have power and gain control over humanity? Were they destined to be wiped off the face of the Earth just because their holistic cures were more effective than those who claimed to be studied, doctors? Were they supposed to be punished because they were intelligent women who refused to be nobodies? They had enough. Their animal ego metaphorically sat like a devil on their shoulders, urging them to devise a solution and stop the madness.

The Wise Women came together to debate (once again) on how to save their kind. They rekindled ancient rituals, awakened full soul power energies, and used this energy against those harming their families. It was like unleashing a caged beast.

In modern days, you may describe it as sending powerful curses against the dark side to stop what they were doing. The Wise Women worked together in unity. They disliked using their power to harm, yet they felt as if there was no other choice. Imagine how powerful they were. If this resonates with you, realize that you were one of them during your life. Imagine the energy curses you were able to conjure. Illness, mental confusion, accidents, bodily harm, poverty, lack of love, and being hunted by demons were a few of the curses sent toward those walking on the dark side. Remember that you did this out of despair, not because you wanted to, but because you felt there was no other way. You felt limited.

KARMA AND CURSES

There is a difference between the energies of karma and those of curses.

Karma often manifests in your life depending on what you have done. For example, bad karma would be created if you were a thief in a past life and stole money from the poor. In this lifetime, you may be the victim of theft, or a money scheme perpetrated by someone you thought was a friend. You may lose a lot of money before the crime is discovered and the culprit captured and imprisoned. You may be satisfied that justice was served, but ultimately, and despite the outcome of this scenario, your job is to forgive this person and yourself for being in that situation. This energy of forgiveness goes back into your soul karma, which heals you. Once you are healed and freed of this negative karma, you will never have to repeat this scenario again, and you may now gain everlasting abundance that is earned with honesty and integrity.

Another thing with karma is that you currently live in a supportive energy period, which allows you to become conscious of your karma. You can consciously step out of your karmic debt and wipe it clean with the promise to live an honest life. It is that easy.

Curses are a different story. A curse you perform is part of your soul power energy that you still give away to do harm. Now, please listen to this with neutral emotions. It is time to forgive and heal. Saying that they deserved it will not justify it in this lifetime. Curses work like boomerangs. It will come back to you as a horrible blockage, obstacle, dark energy, or entity that you may think someone sent to ruin your life. Imagine that the negative energy you sent to attack someone approximately 400 years ago is attacking you back. Every time you cleanse it, it goes back to the intended victim, but it will return to you again in a matter of time. It travels with you from lifetime to lifetime and will travel with you until you release it.

You agreed to fully awaken to regain your soul power/knowledge in your current lifetime. Your soul power/knowledge is within your soul, guarded by your higher self. It is not in your current body. You hid it. To find it, you must forgive and heal your soul, and only then will you be able to retrieve it.

NEW DAWN

Eventually, the Wise Women came to realize the truth of ancient wisdom.

You cannot win a fight with power vs. power. It will only bring temporary relief until the other side refreshes its power. You create an endless cycle of conflicts and suffering. Only unconditional love can bring healing to everything and end the cycle.

In the early beginning of the 16th century, the remaining leaders of the Wise Women tribes were called together to rethink their strategy on how to stop the inhumane killings. The curses worked, but they were not strong enough to stop all of the dark side. Sadly, they knew they could not win this fight. This time, they meditated and asked God's consciousness to guide them. Unfortunately, the planetary alignment energy was unfavorable for a global embrace of unconditional love. It was channeled from the highest Source that they should shut down their power. This meant dimming their soul light into an almost non-existent spark of light to confuse the dark side and buy themselves time until the next stellar activation cycle. This would stop the witch hunts and would protect their souls from more damage.

We would like you to meditate briefly and go back approximately 400 years. Feel the regained trust in God from these remaining Wise Women, who agreed to close their energy instead of demanding super-powered weapons to eliminate the dark side.

Were they angry about what was happening and felt powerless? YES! Were new weapons the answer? NO! You know the saying, "Be the better person, and stop." So, instead of trying to figure out a way to destroy their enemy, they trusted that love would prevail, and they all took a leap of faith. YOU TOOK A LEAP OF FAITH, and YOU outwitted the dark side.

HIDING THE ESSENCE OF YOUR BEING

One trait that the Children of the Law of One were recognized by was that they were the living embodiment of truth; they could not consciously lie or cheat. They could conceal their powers and abilities so well that if one of them walked by you at the market, you would never know you had a master walking beside you. However, their moral compass of the embodiment of truth gave them away when they encountered a soul crying for help.

Closing their light temporarily prevented them from their natural desire to help others. They asked their higher self to hold their soul power (knowledge) hidden within so they could not access it. Imagine locking it in an impenetrable safe and throwing away the key. They had to relinquish their way of being the embodiment of truth to temporarily disable their moral compass (alien compass).

Remember that they were you before this incarnation, and you fully trusted God and your higher self to remind you where to find your locked knowledge when the time was right. For that to happen, you created a personal symbol, your soul symbol, that only your soul would recognize. It would represent the truth for you. This soul symbol became the energy that you left buried in the Earth. You call this the Christ consciousness, which is waiting for you on Earth. The soul symbol is the key to your impenetrable safe, where your soul power is hidden.

Why do you have to find the key first?

When you are the embodiment of truth, you will never abuse the knowledge you have. One who knows the universal truth and is on the Path of Light is willing to serve the souls ready for help.

ENTERING THE UNCONSCIOUS YEARS

The sisters and brothers of the Children of the Law of One (the Wise Women) came together one last time. They held hands around a massive fire and looked into each other's eyes. They felt unconditional love for one another and knew that after the ritual to close the essence of their beings, they would each walk separate paths in different parts of the world. They would forget about each other and pass away alone. They knew it would take several hundreds of years to consciously recognize one another again. Tears rolled down their cheeks as they chanted under the night sky for one last time. Their hearts were wrenched, yet the brave men and women did what seemed impossible. They took the essence of their light beings, sent their knowledge to their higher selves, and buried their symbols in the Earth. This happened spontaneously in several places on Earth.

For about the past 400 years, you have gone through several unconscious lifetimes. You may have been a prostitute, bank robber, soldier, or someone more favorable, such as a farmer, teacher, music composer, etc. The point is that you have experienced many lifetimes that you would not have chosen before you closed your light. If you remember something negative or unfavorable from these past lives, forgive yourself. Remember, you can walk out of your karmic debt by being conscious.

Handfuls were awakened earlier to become lighthouses and to leave you bits and pieces of information you could build on (such as Edgar Cayce, Bill Grey, or Ruth Montgomery, to name just a few from the early 19th century).

The next stellar activation cycle passed in 2012, but the soul call went out earlier than planned (in 1945) when a nuclear explosion was experienced. No advanced technology should be weaponized, and we all became concerned about the future of the Earth.

THE STORY YOU HAVE NOT HEARD

Life's journey has many exciting twists and turns. Just as twin flames are meant to meet one another in this lifetime to transcend their wanting into surrender and acceptance, you were born to meet those who harmed you so that you can forgive them and yourself. Only YOU can stop your boomerang of curses.

We guarantee that you will or already have met your enemy in this lifetime. You may realize that your friend in this lifetime may have been your inquisitor in a past life. Maybe you are married to your enemy, or he/she came as your child. Perhaps a stranger did a random act of kindness for you that saved your life. Yet you sense there is something you need to resolve with these people. The Universe is bringing you back together to make amends so that you both find peace in your soul. These people have already paid their karmic debts. All of you have suffered enough.

And you may ask, how does someone become an inquisitor? Were they born with a taste to torture, to kill, or to rape? The answer is no. Life's circumstances shaped them into who they became. What if someone offered you that horrible job, and you said no? They might tell you they would kill your sister, mother, wife, or your family if you chose not to do the job. What would you choose? The Sons of Belial targeted not only one person but also whole families. Fear is a compelling control tactic. Once someone accepted the position, they had no choice but to learn to cope with it or die. It is a programmed survival mechanism. Many committed suicides. It did not help. You may start out doing something you detest, and you may end up finding pleasure in it. Once again, it is a survival mechanism. Remember the Annunaki and the Blood Oath? The program is in your blood until you revoke it. Fear, control, pleasure.

As if that was not enough, they also made you betray one another. They tortured you until you falsely identified your sister as a witch. What if someone held a knife to your child's throat and asked you to call out your sister or your best friend as a witch? Who would you choose to die? Tough question.

Why do we bring this up? Not only did they commit unspeakable crimes against the loved ones that you pointed out as witches, but when you were no longer of any value to them, they would do the same to you. They would force your sister or best friend to betray you, and she, too, would be forced to stand there and look you in the eye as you were tortured and put to death. You hated her for betraying you and maybe even cursed her with your last dying breath as she watched with a broken heart, all the time hating herself for what she had done. No wonder you feel you cannot trust anyone and prefer to seclude yourself. Who can you trust?

You can trust yourself and have a choice to open your circle again to your sisters and brothers. Forgive them. Forgive them. Forgive them. You were all manipulated.

In conclusion, you grew weary of all the upheaval and persecutions around the twelfth century. You decided to stop following God and took faith into your own hands. By the sixteenth century, you had no strength to continue, and you closed off your light and stopped living the life you were meant to live.

There is no judgment in our words—only unconditional love. We feel your pain. We hear your soul calling for help. What you started had to end, and you did. You are the bravest of the brave! Now, it is time to continue. Are you ready to do it your way, or are you prepared to follow God? What is ahead for you?

THE PATH TO HEALING

Forgiveness, unconditional love (of the soul), and light (happiness of the mind) are the components of the trinity that you need to assist you in releasing the curses, negative thoughts, and wishes you had sent out during times of desperation.

Since this was done in a ritual, we recommend you use a ritual now as well. Rituals help you focus your thoughts and your energy. If you feel overwhelmed by emotion the first time you do this, give yourself some time. Be gentle with yourself. Repeat this anytime you meet someone who you think may have been an inquisitor or someone who you or your family during your previous lifetimes. Only YOU can stop your boomerang and free your soul.

THE REVOCATION OF CURSES

Prepare three white candles. Tealight candles are fine, but any will do. Mediate with your intentions.

The first candle represents everything from the past. It is to forgive everyone who has ever harmed you or your family. It is to forgive yourself for being in that situation.

The second candle represents the present and your conscious decision to release all curses and negative energy. It is for unconditional love, the highest available energy that will release all curses, negative thoughts, and wishes. Send unconditional love to those who harmed you or your family. Fill them with unconditional love, and fill yourself with unconditional love. Unconditional love is selfless love, love without conditions. Your soul is fully capable of having this level of love.

The third candle represents your future. It is for light, to illuminate the Path of Light for all those that you have forgiven. They can see the light and walk that path if they choose. This light will also illuminate the same path for you.

Since you have forgiven and released the curses with your soul's unconditional love, the light you are invoking is a twin flame of your soul-mind consciousness that can create the happiest reality you desire.

When you are ready, light each candle while saying your revocation. Mean and feel it; speak from your heart, not your mind; otherwise, you simply say empty words.

First candle:
By the power of three,
I forgive thee.

(This means people who harmed you, your family, your friends, and yourself.)

Second candle:
By the power of unconditional love,
I heal our soul wounds,
And, I release all the curses I have sent in any time and space.
(Unconditional love is more vital than any curse or death and will stop the boomerang effect.)

Third candle:
By the power of light,
I illuminate the light within,
For us all,
To shine on the path,
Toward a new life.
(Darkness and fear within no longer have the power to intimidate you.)

After your ritual, take a few days to reflect on how far you have come and what comes next for you. Nothing is holding you back anymore. Your soul's mission in this lifetime was to heal, and you accomplished that. What is next? What would you like to do? How can you be of service?

FINDING YOUR SOUL SYMBOL

Only you will know when you are ready for this.
Practice staying neutral in your emotions every day.
1. Build a safe nest for your ego and your physical
being (as described in Chapter 6). Tell yourself often
that it is safe to embrace your gifts once again.
2. Quiet your mind, meditate, and practice being one
with the Universe. Set your judgment aside, and
question your fears as they are clues to what needs to
be healed.
3. Practice trusting your higher self and God. Perhaps
you need to have a good conversation with God to
discuss and let out how betrayed and angry you feel.
Then, listen with your heart as unconditional love pours
in.
4. Ask that you remember your soul symbol and pay
attention to signs and synchronicity in your life. The
odds are that you have already seen your symbol many
times; you did not consciously recognize it then. You
will know when you find it. You will have an "AHA"
moment, and many doors will open.

Once you re-discover what your soul symbol is (it
can be a number, a geometric shape, a picture, it can be
in a physical shape or etheric), take or imagine your
soul symbol and practice this little exercise:

1. Make a firm decision that you are done suffering. Review your life and be honest with yourself. See what worked and what did not. Once again, if need be, forgive yourself and others. Take what you have learned and use it as a strong foundation. You have learned A LOT in this lifetime and in the past.

When you define your foundation (what made you who you are today), accept it and fill yourself with unconditional love. Love every moment of your life, good days and bad days.

2. Put one hand, palm facing down, on your belly button (3rd chakra) and the other facing down on your throat (5th chakra). Say these words and FEEL them (feel the emotions) in your body. You need to feel the energy of these words—the words are empty if the energy from your emotions is not in them.

I live the truth!   (3rd chakra)

I speak the truth!   (5th chakra)

I am the embodiment of the truth!   (4th chakra)

Then, exchange the hands in a clockwise motion. The one on your belly button will now be on your throat and vice versa. Repeat this. Take your time. Breathe through the words and FEEL THEM.

Next, put both palms on your heart as the last step and breathe this symbol in. Merge with your symbol and accept it as part of you.

3. Imagine this symbol traveling to your higher self (it is your key) to unlock the knowledge that your higher self has been storing for you for hundreds of years. Your symbol becomes one with your higher self and then integrate with your physical body. (Key + Soul Knowledge) Your symbol brings missing knowledge of your soul into your physical body. You are whole. Imagine standing by the fire with your sisters and brothers and taking back what you have hidden away for so long.

When you do this honestly from your heart, you will embark on a new journey. You will perform all physical tasks with honesty and integrity (I live the truth!). You will always express yourself truthfully without lies or empty promises (I speak the truth!). You will become your true self, and the door to the ancient truths and all possibilities will be open for you. You will embody the frequency of truth (I am the embodiment of the truth!). Your spark will ignite others.

In conclusion, releasing curses will stop the boomerang effect that causes blockages to return to your life. Finding your soul symbol will open a door into the ancient wisdom library hidden within your higher self. This is the way back home. Sometimes, you have to retrace your steps and mend the broken pieces of your soul to find the true essence of your being so that you can move forward in your journey.

CHAPTER 11

THE QUANTUM FIELD OF LIMITLESS POSSIBILITIES

"The future is not set in stone. It is in your hands." ~
Pleiadians

Trust is the key, while inner guidance is the map into the quantum field of limitless possibilities. You can choose to live in this quantum field while trusting that everything will align the way it needs to be. When you trust, you are not controlling the outcome. The outcome will be a divine product of your trust.

Now we ask you, after all you have endured, will you open yourself again for another journey of possibilities? Will you feel safe reclaiming your soul symbol? Will you trust the knowledge that your higher self will share with you? Will you trust divine guidance?

If your answer is "Yes," then we are on this path beside you, surrounding you with unconditional love.

Reflect on your past. There were times when your lack of trust led to failure. However, the lifetimes in which you did trust divine guidance will not present themselves as obstacles. Memories of these lifetimes are deeply hidden within you, like a valuable old book concealed in the darkest corner of a library. These memories will remain dormant until you are ready to recall them. They are linked to divine guidance so you can comprehend their true significance. For instance, the Emerald Tablets will only be helpful once you are prepared to interpret them with an enlightened mind rather than your human ego's mind.

NEXT STEP

When you neutralize your ego, you make it your ally instead of your narcissistic protector. Healing your past lives and soul wounds will put you at number 8 in the Fibonacci sequence. You are becoming God. You are one step away from reaching the Surrogate God crystal and one step closer to removing your anchor.

The original life plan was designed to prevent you from reaching this step while still in your body. Doing so could have been seen as a threat by the Sons of Belial, as they may have believed you had figured out their dark schemes. However, the rules have changed. You are now living in a lifetime of incredible spiritual support that was developed to help you remember who you truly are. This may allow some of you to reach this level of consciousness while still in the physical body.

The Sons of Belial knew that the future was not set in stone. It can always be changed. Because of this (once you become conscious), the dark side will tempt you with false gifts, false prophecies, and false channeling so you will feel either superior or afraid or as if you are chasing something that you will never find, instead of staying humble, neutral and on your path.

Do not fool yourself. There is not, and will not, be a second coming. You ALL are IT. Christ is within you. You are the creators, and you are seeding the new humanity. The new humanity is seeded not from the seeds you grow in the garden or that someone will ship you via priority mail but through your activated light codes of your higher soul-mind consciousness. When YOU change, you become a "new" human being. You have become a new human being when you pass the "three trap doors" (described in chapter 3) while staying humble, trusting the divine guidance, and setting your inner GPS toward serving humanity. When people want to be like you, living in honesty, integrity, and from the heart with unconditional love, you will be the master seeder of a new human race.

Superiority is only temporary. The dark side will discard you once they no longer need you. You will fall, and you will blame God. You will believe that "he" does not help you, that "he" does not love you, that "he" lets you suffer, and that "he" betrayed you. This has happened many times in the past. Is God this "he" you refer to? Who are you really blaming? Are you too afraid to acknowledge that you have been misled by something you thought was God because it made your human ego feel good and you temporarily had "what you" wanted?

God is neither a man nor a woman. In your dimension, God is the vastness of unconditional love. God is peace without a form, color, sound, or emotion in higher dimensions. It just is. This "it" created many solar systems, each different, to give your soul the experiences it desires.

RECALLING YOUR MEMORIES

You may have dreams, glimpses, or an unexplained obsession with finding Atlantis. Imagine fully remembering when you were an extraterrestrial or recalling your knowledge of advanced technology.

The memory of Jesus Christ is still alive after over 2,000 years. Think of what you can accomplish once you awaken Christ's consciousness.

You still use herbal remedies despite what happened to you when you were one of the Wise Women. Imagine how much you will be able to help others once you fully recall all the medical knowledge locked within you and how to use it to cure illness like you used to in ancient times.

These are your three main past lives; there are many others, but these caused the most damage to your soul. Now that you know how to heal your soul, you can consciously and safely recall memories. You are a descendant of the ancient Atlanteans. You are not occupying the same body you had in Atlantis, but you still have the same soul. You re-incarnated in physical bodies of all different colors, sexes, sexual orientations, faiths, religions, etc. Why? Because humans keep separating themselves and pointing fingers at each other, thinking that one belief is better than another. Because humans grow apart faster than they grow together. You came to fix all that and help build the foundation for a new, better humanity.

New Human

After reaching and stabilizing yourself at Fibonacci sequence number 8, you will explore the numbers 13 and 21. You will undergo several re-births while your new human defines its new personality. The new you will utilize your ancestral DNA while living in a human vessel. The new you will be able to live between the third and fifth dimensions without effort, as your ancestors did. The new you will live from the heart (not the mind) and effectively use telepathy, empathy, clairaudience, clairsentience, etc. The new you will be able to connect to the universal mind and create new inventions to make the Earth a better place.

The Mayans left you a gift before leaving your dimension: They created the calendar, which ended in 2012. You are now in a period of new beginnings, during which you can become fully aware of your ancient abilities and create limitless possibilities to alter your reality. Alternatively, you may choose to repeat history and start again at the beginning.

-   If you create from the level of fear, you will create a fear-based reality.
-   You will create a limited-based reality if you create from a limited perception.
-   If you create from "what you want and what you think is best for this world," you will create a dictator-based reality controlled by one person (despite the fact that your intentions are positive in your mind). What may sound favorable to you may sound controlling to someone else.
-   If you fully set your personal needs aside and trust the divine guidance, you will create from unconditional love, an unconditional love–based reality. It will not be the same reality for all of you, but it will vary according to everyone's needs. Everyone will be happy. For example, carnivores will eat their steak for dinner, while vegetarians will enjoy their spinach quiche. Both will be happy instead of judging one another.

Unconditional love is the highest type of frequency for the physical body. Love is like a magic potion. Love is the essence of every miracle. Love turns the impossible into the likely. Love is blind. Love is breathtaking. We all ultimately desire love, despite what side we are on (whether dark or light). We opened this book with a love story and will end it with one:

The Son of Belial fell in love with the Daughter of the Children of the Law of One. A twin flame of love was ignited, and hope was born. They put their differences aside and saw each other as something they each missed within. They completed one another and made each other whole. They let go of their individual dreams and found harmony in their new goal of creating a Heaven on Earth by becoming frequency holders for unconditional love.

They embarked on a journey of mutual ancestral healing. Together, they learned that no one is better than the other and that there was no need to blame anyone regarding the past. Ancestral healing created a catalyst in their life. Spiritual and monetary abundance was poured into their life. Looking at them, they embodied happiness and respect for one another. They decided to open a spiritual center to assist others in their transformation. Ancient knowledge was taught with unconditional love, and everyone followed the center's rules. Those two became living examples for others to follow, creating a life that humans desire.

Challenges were raised when they became too busy with the growing number of seekers who came to their spiritual center to learn. Some seekers succeeded in transforming, but those whose egos failed and could not transform blamed the Son of Belial and Daughter of the Children of the Law of One for their failures.

The Son of Belial and Daughter of the Children of the Law of One trusted one another and followed the divine guidance. They knew that they could not help those whose souls were not ready. Instead of being upset, they often communicated their feelings with one another and supported each other with unconditional love. They were balanced and wise, but they were getting old. By the end of their lifetime, they had healed their souls. They were ready to disconnect their energy from the Surrogate God crystal and return home. Their spiritual center was well established with true teachers that they trained so that new seekers could continue learning after they were gone.

Their cycle was completed. One night, as they lay in their bed, they held each other's hands and simultaneously knew that they were ready for their next journey. When their souls left their bodies, they rejoiced with happiness. This time, their healed souls soared very high and did not get trapped in 4D Heaven. Instead, they went to spend some time with their soul families on Orion and Pleiades before starting their new journey of being one with the Universe. Their Earth journey had ended.

We love you unconditionally ~ The Pleiadians

About The Author

Eva Marquez is a spiritual consultant, soul healer, guide, teacher, TM Sidha, and writer with a Pleiadian starseed lineage. She has authored six books and appeared on Gaia TV's "Beyond Belief." She works alongside her guides, the Lights of the Universe, a group of light beings from different star nations, including the Pleiades. In her spiritual practice, she draws on Pleiadian energy, the Language of Light, and other ancient soul memories.

Eva and her team help starseeds remember their past lives on Earth and beyond, activate their dormant cosmic DNA, and reconnect with their soul family. She strives to aid starseeds in adapting to their physical bodies, empowering them to fulfill their life missions in supporting humanity's evolution into a multidimensional species while safeguarding the planet for future generations.

Eva brings the memories of infinite love – the essence of God's Source – the most profound energy that is your original essence. She walks beside you on your life journey, assisting you in letting go of your fears of darkness and limitations and seeing the light at the end of the tunnel. Ultimately, she guides you to the point where infinite love is no longer a memory but your guide. Infinite love will become your friend on the journey toward the light of your origin. Love and light give birth to the wisdom that is a compass for the soul-mind consciousness on the healing journey of returning home to its original source. It is Eva's greatest wish that you find your way home.

Learn more about Eva and her services and classes:
www.EvaMarquez.org

Visit Eva's YouTube channel: Eva Marquez

OTHER BOOKS BY EVA MARQUEZ

ONE LAST THING

If you liked this book, I would be grateful if you could leave a brief review on Amazon. Your support means a lot to me, and I read every review. Thank you for being so supportive!

Love and Light,
Eva Marquez